QUEST BY CANOE
GLASGOW TO SKYE

By
ALASTAIR M. DUNNETT

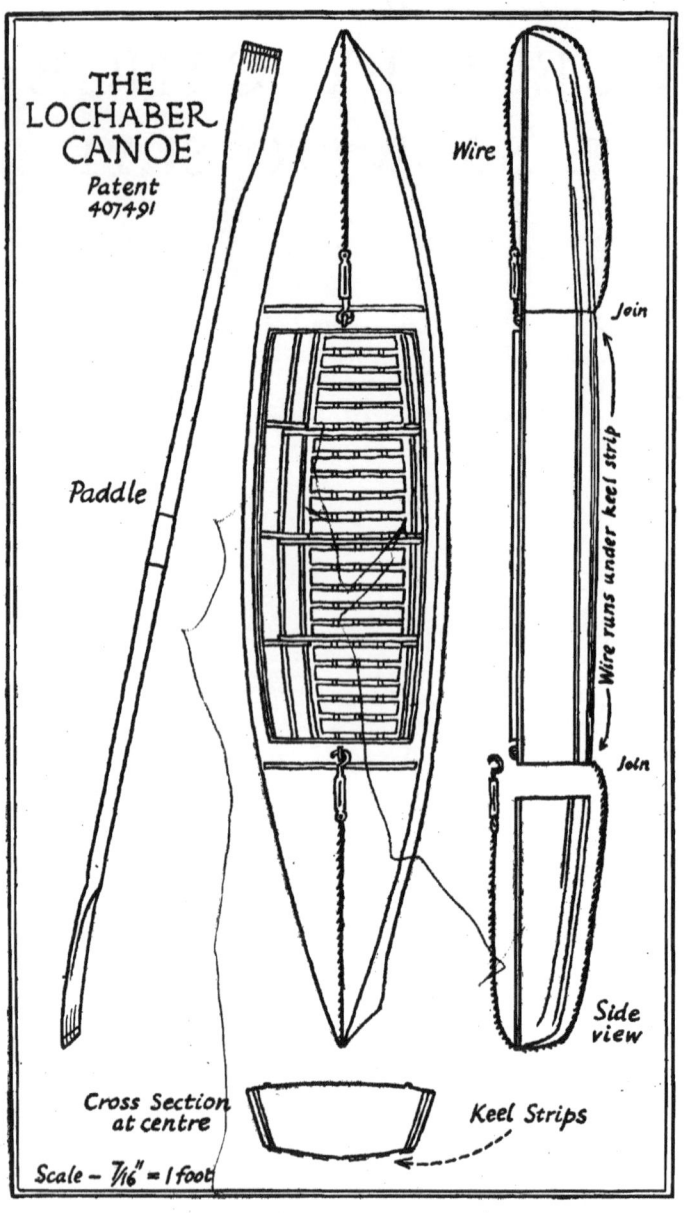

CONTENTS

CHAPTER		PAGE
I.	FAILURE	1
II.	'CHANGE!'	9
III.	THE START	15
IV.	JOURNEY WITH A MELON	23
V.	THE KINSMAN	34
VI.	THE DORUS MOR	47
VII.	THE ISLES	56
VIII.	SEA CANOEING	69
IX.	THE SPANISH ARMADA	78
X.	FAMILY FARM	91
XI.	ARDMORE	104
XII.	THE FORBIDDEN ISLAND	117
XIII.	THE HIGHLAND PROBLEM	132
XIV.	THE HERRING FISHERS	145
XV.	NORTHWARD	160
XVI.	THE HIGHLAND PROBLEM RESOLVED	172
XVII.	'IT'S TOO LATE IN THE YEAR'	181

ILLUSTRATIONS

		FACING PAGE
1. THE START. *Daily Sketch* photograph		24
2. DEPARTURE FROM BOWLING. Photograph by R. MacLean		25
3. OUR FIRST NIGHT OUT. Photograph by R. MacLean		25
4. THE CRINAN CANAL SEA-LOCKS. Photograph by W. S. Thomson of Fort William		40
5. THE ATLANTIC BRIDGE AT CLACHAN. Photograph by W. S. Thomson		41
6. EASDALE SEEN FROM DUN MOR ON SEIL. Photograph by W. S. Thomson		72
7. SEUMAS AT STORNOWAY. Author's photograph		73
8. PACKING UP A CANOE. By courtesy of Eneas Mackay, publisher		73
9. BACK OF KEPPOCH, NEAR ARISAIG. Photograph by W. S. Thomson		88
10. CALVE ISLAND. Author's photograph		89
11. HEBRIDEANS. Photograph by James S. Adam		89
12. THE DESERTED FARM AT ARDMORE. Author's photograph		104
13. THE CEILIDH BAND AT CALVE. Author's photograph		104
14. THE AUTHOR AT ARDMORE. Author's photograph		105
15. RHUM SEEN BEYOND EIGG. Photograph by A. D. S. Macpherson		120
16. OUR LAST CAMP ON EIGG. Author's photograph		121
17. A MALLAIG KIPPERING SHED. Author's photograph		121
18. THE FRINGES OF ARDTOE HAMLET. Photograph by W. S. Thomson		136
19. PEAT-CUTTING IN SKYE. Photograph by W. S. Thomson		137
20. VIEW FROM ELGOL IN SKYE. Photograph by A. D. S. Macpherson		152
21. THE 'GOLDEN EMBLEM' LEAVES MALLAIG. Author's photograph		153
22. THE AUTHOR LEAVING MALLAIG		153

CHAPTER I

FAILURE

> Only who stand and wait
> The conquered are.
> There is more than one gate
> And none ajar.
> The road is still straight—
> But it goes far.

THE *Claymore* ceased publication in the second week of July, at the urgent request of our printer. He was by far our largest and most patient creditor, and in the end it took us six years to pay him off. Putting the last number to press, we went to bed in our bare, single-roomed office in York Place, Edinburgh, and slept almost uninterruptedly for two days. During this time there came through the letter-box four progressively swelling cascades of dunning letters, appeals from bereft readers, and the August sales orders which we could not now fulfil. The postman, who for many weeks had been no messenger of joy, would have been scantily interested to learn that behind the door which he assaulted twice daily with foreboding handfuls of mail, there lay asleep and exhausted two stickit press lords.

Seumas Adam and I had founded the *Claymore* because there had to be a *Claymore* and no one else had thought of starting it. It was a tuppenny weekly adventure paper for Scottish boys, and none of the robust excitements it gave its readers ever matched the weekly adventure of its continued being. There was nothing of frivolity, however, in its creation. Seumas* and I were only two of many, then and since, who have hoped to play some part in the re-forming of a scattered Scottishness. It was clear that, being very young and without influence, our best chance of influencing anything at all lay in a long-term directing of our effort at the boys who would be men in ten years.

We had always found it easy to stimulate in Scottish boys an

---

* The name should be pronounced Shay-mas.

interest in Scotland. This was rarely even an incidental aim of schools or youth organisations, and we had the field to ourselves. Our 'prentice hand had already laboured in this urgent domestic cause, with gratifying results. Working within the Boy Scout movement in the West of Scotland, we had wiped out from its self-conscious mythology most of the Red Indian cult, substituting for it authentic and healthy elements from the outdoor traditions of the country where the youngsters had their roots. Boys became clansmen, because that was in fact what they were. They saved up to buy a kilt of their clan tartan. They found out what was happening to their clan territories to-day. They went camping on clan ground and grew to a warm kinship with the land and the folk on it. Not one of them was the worse for it, nor longed to be a cowboy or a Blackfoot. We saw them grow up strongly, and their minds with them, and knew it was time to put this operation into practice on a large scale.

No range of Scottish periodicals existed. There was consequently little market for the Scots writer who cared to depart from the stock view of his country and its people. The only possible sustaining force of any people is the virtue of patriotism, with as many separate gradations of appeal as there are citizens. In Scotland in the nineteen-thirties this was a gravely spent force. For adults there existed a narrow choice of opportunities for national fervour—crude enough, but something to be going on with until the country could be shocked out of its second childhood and drawn to a mature focus. There was Para Handy; the Glasgow Comedians; international football occasions at Hampden and Murrayfield. Extracts from this list could bring to mind the zest, if not altogether the dignity, of the place to which they belonged; where most of them would live, work, and see out the end of their days.

But for the children there was not even this short group of enthusiasms, while their literature painted a greatly different scene. The boys' weekly papers already in existence had a wide range of stimulus. They led their readers adventuring into all parts of the globe—except one. The somewhat repetitive pattern of their tales dealt with young explorers up the Amazon or down the Congo; South Sea planters' sons; English boy football stars; pet gorillas which played cricket; jabbering and excited foreigners ready to be cowed by clean-cut types; Zulu chiefs who would eagerly exchange herds of cattle for alarm clocks. Only one part of the world did not pulse with these thrills. The weekly wave of adventure never reached the Scottish shore: not even on the home front, which was held to be adequately covered by stories of English public school life. In this grand pattern of events no British schoolboy could hope to be a hero unless he had been a fag and a Fourth Former in his day, with plenty of high-class japes. The 'bad yins' of these tales, apart from an occasional genteel cad, were coarse errand lads, usually discovered twisting the arms of small boys, although these villainies were mere by-products of the major crime of working for a living.

It is generally agreed, although in another context, that the mind holds to impressions regularly received in youth. I believe that the power of early influence over the youthful mind can be greatly exaggerated. However, we came to the conclusion at the time that these literary enticements were likely to overbalance all but the most sturdy, and that Scots boys were bound to grow up with a tendency to regard themselves as potential emigrants or *déclassé* provincials.

I find that I am mentioning these trends in the past tense, as if all the evils that poisoned a nation's hope and future have since been overcome. They have not, but the air is a little clearer. At the time of the *Claymore*'s founding we were not the only ones with a mission of print. Many propagandists were writing, and even precariously publishing. There was plenty to complain of in Scotland's situation, although the cause has since become more fashionable. Anger stirred ink into a flow of white-hot inspiration, and some of the pamphleteering of these days was as mordantly brilliant as any patriotic situation has ever called forth. But there was no laughter—no wit. Conceived in such a grim passion, the issue was bound to be humourless. We believed that this technique was wrong for anybody, but it was certainly wrong for us.

We gave to our readers a picture of Scotland as a Land of Adventure. It was a staggering novelty, but they stood up to it bravely, and in growing numbers. Here was a robust, modern, and above all cheery setting for the whole gamut. The story themes were inexhaustible. If one wanted football stars—where were there any better? In a country which had invented so many sports, the sports theme was a natural fit. Schools?—Rookwood and Greyfriars were sissy retreats from the authentic vigour of Tayside, our fictional *Alma Mater*. And so through the list. It is tempting at this remove to smile at the amateurism which may have been visible. The fact is that the stuff was good. Much of it was later produced in book form by publishers who knew their business. The *Claymore* was sent, at their request, to various libraries and exhibitions throughout the world and put on show as the selected example of the British tuppenny for youths. This prestige had ruefully little cash value. We could have been doing with the tuppences.

For a number of reasons (one of them paramount), most of the work was unpaid, written by our two selves, or by a small group of our Glasgow friends who gave all their spare time to the effort. 'I'd live on brose for a year to put this over,' said one of them. Two of the most eminent artists in the boys' periodical market drew illustrations for us anonymously. It was their first opportunity to do intelligent work in the juvenile fiction field. Their own firm insisted on a trashy quality of drawing, while we, with standards unrelated to finance, insisted that even their best was hardly good enough for *Claymore* readers.

All through the first winter and the spring we held our own. We had settled to a sales level which, in a normal publishing concern, would have been a healthy foundation on which to build circulation. But our publishing activities were far from normal. Seumas and I had given up our jobs to devote our full time to the affair, and full time it truly turned out to be. My job, incidentally, had been the safest in the world—on the staff of the Commercial Bank of Scotland's head office. Seumas had been East of Scotland advertisement manager of a national newspaper. We had not attempted to borrow money, but had launched away on our own savings. This made a laughably small total which we were later convinced our publisher had probably misheard in our conversations as the figure he might expect from us each week, instead of the total capital resources of the new power in the world of publishing.

We had also to eat and sleep, if infrequently. To accomplish this within the narrow margin of profit which was to be expected initially, we moved into an inexpensive but undeniably literary lodging in Forrest Road, near the University of Edinburgh, sharing the room, with meals, at a straining limit of a pound apiece per week. This outlay soon proved to be extravagant, and one night we stole away from these comforts to the spot amenities of our office room, where we lived until the end of the chapter, unsuspected by our landlord. We slept on camp beds, cooked on a gas ring such food as it was expedient to come by, and eventually cut down our living costs to an all-in figure of ten shillings a week for the two of us.

Bread, oatmeal brose and lentil soup were the cheap main items of our food, and although I shall later be describing with gusto the part played by brose in our canoe trip, it tends to be a colourless regular diet for indoor workers. Not that we noticed this much at the time, for the day's jobs were spiced with variety. At least once in most weeks we found it possible to resort to an unseemly small eating-house near Canonmills, where soup cost a penny per well-thumbed plate, and an entire lunch was procurable for eightpence.

From time to time, however, hunger made us bold, and once it sent us plainly begging. We walked into the most expensive café in Princes Street with the sum of one-and-threepence between us. In the pre-*Claymore* days we had often dined in this gay scene, with its palms, gilt, discreet orchestra, and high-priced food. Our main interest in the place was in its young and efficient manageress, a daughter of Skye with the mien of a princess. We had been accustomed to install ourselves in a corner, send up to the orchestra requests for unusual musical items, and carry on a conversation with the manageress in our pidgin-Gaelic. But these were the former times. Now we arrived cadaverously, went straight to her, and said: 'Eisd, Sandy!' (for that was really her name) 'We're hungry—and we've only got one-and-three.' Sandy gave orders without a tremor; food came in profusion, and at the end the bill was a shilling, so that on leaving we were able to tip the waitress.

It soon appeared that these economies were not enough. We were by now working eighteen hours out of the twenty-four, what with writing, editing, and the absorbing but exacting incidentals of circulation, and publicity matters, office correspondence, competitions and the despatch of prizes, the delivery of parcels, the avuncular receiving of enthusiastic readers calling in person, and the multitude of other tasks which one has since seen rather less intensively spread about a staff of some hundreds, and experts at that.

To augment our subsistence income we turned to the writing of articles for more settled publications, finding the sleeping hours of one or two nights per week the most suitable, because the only, time for these extra outpourings. I wrote a serial novel for a national weekly newspaper, and appeared smirking sleepily in a photograph bravely reproduced by our adult contemporary, whose money was welcome. No juvenile paper has ever experienced anything like the sudden effusion of display advertising which we carried in the *Claymore*. These were captured by Seumas in a dogged burst of space-selling genius. The advertisers got their money's worth, for we picked them, and not they us, and by this time we had the most fervent readership of any youth newspaper of our size in the business.

By the middle of the summer we were going down heavily. An annual phenomenon of which we were unaware—the reluctance of youths to read in the summer—punished our hard-won circulation. We had no resources on which to lean until the winter should bring round again the benison of eager readership. Staving off the crisis, we found time for personal canvassing on the tenement stairs of Edinburgh, trusting that in our door-to-door salesmanship we should not encounter any of the readers we had already met in the rôle of editor. Many busy mothers, pausing on their doorsteps in forenoon conversation with us, filled up the form which ensured for their sons, with our eager guarantee, elevating yet virile reading matter. We salute these matrons across the years. Our Glasgow allies took a part, on their own territory, in these sale-getting efforts. Two of them, pursued by policemen, carried out a number of middle-of-the-night fly-posting sorties, leaving *Claymore* bills stuck on prominent unpaid sites. A borrowed motor-bike played a large part in these raids, with the pillion passenger clasping a damp bundle of bills, already pasted, and ready to be clapped glutinously on the target.

But it was not enough. We were losing money weekly in formidable sums, and our printer, knowing that we had long since said Good-bye to the petty initial finance, was coming to the warrantable conclusion that the money we were losing was his. He used to summon the pallid proprietors to his office in search of reassurance, and there was no one to whom we would more willingly have offered this diminishing commodity. We pointed optimistically to the certain profits of the next winter; but our debt to him talked in a louder voice, and by the time the harvest was due the figure would be prodigious. Seumas and I had now nothing to lose but our hopes and our health, and the printer must have noted that the latter asset was also draining away with the rest of the called-up capital. On the whole, the decision to stop printing was doubtless the wisest business course from his point of view.

These events are only the preliminary to the story told here: but they are in a consistent pattern with everything which came after. We were now left without money, heavily in debt, jobless, and in precarious health. Still we were, however, our own masters, and we put this privilege to work at once in day-long indulgence in sleep. One forgets readily a past sense of exhaustion, but neither of us will ever fail to recall the weariness that muscle by muscle, cell by cell, had to be driven out of us. We soaked in sleep, and soon were men again.

Cheques from the wholesale newsagents for the sales of the previous month began to come in, and we laid this little capital aside for a new springboard. We had at once to get back to fitness, and to earn some living. What we needed was some sort of holiday which would pay for itself. For the past year we had been in the habit of creating out of nothing a setting for ourselves, and in a day or two such a situation had emerged again and was being shaped.

Some months earlier we had discovered a manufacturer whose work appeared to be of such adventurous significance that we accorded it the only accolade which lay in our gift—a descriptive story in the *Claymore*. John Marshall of North Queensferry had a genius for design. He had the trick of building things to do a job well. After a recent study of the economy and habits of poultry he had designed a hen-house which won a medal at the Highland Agricultural Show. For some time he had been pondering, at first for his own pleasure, the problems of small boats, and had eventually evolved a light-weight canoe which, he believed, would take a skilly man anywhere in the waters around our coasts in all but the most severe conditions. For his design Marshall had harked back to the low-slung secrets of the

Eskimo kayak, and especially to the more rigid Rob Roy pattern evolved by John MacGregor three generations before our day. With this canoe he had gone into production commercially in sheds beside his home above the Firth of Forth, and at this stage we took him up enthusiastically in the *Claymore*. In the spring of the year, while the paper was still a going concern, we had embarked five of our Glasgow editorial supporters on an eight-day trip among and across the Isles of the Hebrides, and the diary of the trip, with its log of inshore Atlantic voyages, shooting of Uist rapids, portages across the bogs, and aquatic encampments, and especially of encounters with the Isles folk, made a first-rate series of articles on our insistent theme—adventure in Scotland.

It was to the canoes we turned, after the failure of the *Claymore*. The plan took shape quickly—as it had to, for the summer was passing. We would attempt an open-sea voyage from the Clyde to the Outer Isles. The obvious hazards of the trip would no doubt bait enticingly the stories we would write for newspapers, magazines, and the radio. In the course of an adventure story we hoped to tell, this time to adult audiences, something of the urgent purpose of our beliefs. In the doing of it we should expect to become at least as expert as any others in the state and possibilities of those neglected areas, and we believed that, unless the Highland fate was to be planned desolation, this hard-won expertise would be an asset.

Although, if the voyage succeeded, the publicity value to the canoe business would be immense, it would be more than cancelled if we met with disaster—an outcome which, as the best navigational advice quickly pointed out, was only too greatly to be feared. John Marshall, however, co-operated generously from the beginning, and immediately set to the construction of two superb canoes.

But first we had to build up a starting fund of physique. Except in heart, we were sadly stooped and flabby. We looked around for a method of growing hard.

CHAPTER II

'CHANGE!'

> Our steel has rusted in the night;
> We fail, unless we make it good—
> Seek increase of our little might
> And gather up our hardihood.

A SURVEY over the familiar and barren field of our resources brought to light a small asset which might still, we hoped, have a marketable value. At the start of the *Claymore*, Seumas had paid three guineas to Charlie Cotter's Gymnasium in Leith Street. This had entitled him to three hours' physical training per week for a period of ten weeks, the assumption being that he would thereby remain suitably toned up for his new labours. As we have seen, the business of the past year had made derisory the expenditure of three hours per week on mere matters of personal health, and the subscription had lapsed after Seumas had enjoyed only a single week of muscling.

Emboldened by poverty and a winter of selling improbabilities, Seumas went to interview Charlie. He returned hoarse with sales-talking, to announce that Charlie had sportingly agreed to take us both on every day for three weeks, for as many hours as we could stick it. All this for the long-since lapsed balance of the three guineas. It was noble salesmanship, but the most persuasive argument, Seumas admits, was the sight of his own podgy slackness. This deterioration, however, in a measure prepared Charlie for the repellent spectacle of the other half of the contract upon which he had to work—my own meagre frame, stripped and presented bashfully upon the gymnasium floor the next day, when we started. I have lost weight steadily since the age of seventeen, but the process had lately been accelerated, and the skeletal chest against which Charlie thrust a rough ear in the attempt to discern a heart-beat must have appeared the least promising piece of raw material with which the maestro had ever grappled.

Charlie Cotter's Gymnasium is a large single room in a draughty Edinburgh tenement. Here the devotees of physical culture perform their tasks, later to be brutally described, while, in a corner, those released from the agonies stand in a bath and take a punishing shower of icy water. Hot water is not included among the amenities, thus giving point to the only authentic jest in the place. Each time the gymnasts still in the throes hear the hissing of the shower, they beg: 'Don't use all the hot water!' I believe Charlie took a special interest in preparing us for the canoe trip in the hope that he might add us in some way to his gallery of famous pupils, to be quoted to suitably awed newcomers. This list includes such diverse characters as Tancy Lee, Sir Iain Colquhoun, Bart., of Luss, The Duke of Hamilton, Jimmy Guthrie, the T.T. rider, and Albert D. ('MacNib') Mackie, formerly Universities boxing champion at his weight, and lately better known as the Editor of the *Edinburgh Evening Dispatch*. I do hear that we are in fact still quoted furtively among this galaxy, as examples of the extremism to which orthodox training is occasionally subject.

We started, as I have said. The Cotter System is a series of arm, head, neck, shoulder, trunk and leg exercises performed in a non-stop series while holding iron dumb-bells. In cold weather the dumb-bells are heated on a small stove before being handed to the performer. Charlie's excellence is that he knows to a hairbreadth the particular stage beyond the limit of endurance to which a man can be hounded, and still live. He, or his son Richard, would stand us on the floor, say 'Begin!', and leave us nodding and swinging at the first exercise. We carried on with this until long past breaking-point, as it seemed, until at last, when hope had almost gone, would come the welcome word 'Change!' This is the signal, not to pause or rest, but to start on the second exercise. The relief is so pronounced that the movement to the more progressive form of energy is itself a relief. You can always recognise a Cotter pupil in any part of the world if his eyes light up when he hears the word 'Change!' Exhaustion soon creeps deadly along the new muscles until they too are squeaking. In the meantime the man you are paying to do this to you is absently looking out of the window, or massaging a limp figure on a bench. 'In-out, in-out, in-out,' you say to yourself. 'Good God, he's forgotten again! In-out, in-out—hey, I'm dying!

Hey! . . . in-out, in-out . . . I can manage three more . . . in-out, in-out . . . in-out . . . another—another—more . . . in-out, in-out . . .' (until the sweat closes the eyes) '. . . in-out . . . in-out. . . . I'll stop! In-out . . . he's made a mistake this time! . . . In-out, in——' 'Change!' 'Up-down, up-down—cheers, this is wonderful! Slash into it—up-down, up-down, up-down. . . .'

A more refined series of evolutions is performed lying on the back and thrashing the legs in the air in circular and scissors movements. This bears hard on the stomach, an encumbrance with which Seumas was much better endowed than I. It is also a method by which one can come to a rapid dislike of one's legs. They are extremely heavy objects, and look repulsive when airborne, and trembling with the midriff effort which keeps them aloft. Here too the ear craned for the cry of 'Change!', and the stomach muscles—such as they were with us at the time—stood in stringy ridges like breaking spines. It was during one such early session that Seumas drooped his legs painfully to the floor and moaned accusingly: 'Charlie, I've ruptured myself!' Charlie prodded at the area, obviously grudging the halt. 'Ruptured naething!' he said. 'You're just no' gaun' hard enough. On ye go again!'

Leaving the place on the first, second, and third days we hirpled down by the banisters, with our knees impotent. But we hardened quickly, and before half our time was out Charlie was taking well over an hour to tire us thoroughly. We added, as a luxury, the rhythmic hammering of punch-balls, and soon felt our muscles standing out firmly under the grey-sharp needles of the shower. I was filling out, and Seumas was filling in. It was a triumph of the disciplinary hand. By no conceivable process would an individual force himself privately to the effort to which we submitted ourselves at the hands of Charlie Cotter, and it was his skill which brought the canoe trip within our powers. It was to become an act of physique as well as of faith.

All this output of energy disturbed our careful housekeeping. We had to eat more. These August days in Edinburgh were hot and sunny. There was plenty of fruit to be had cheaply, and we ate strawberries at sixpence a pound as a change from dry bread and oatmeal brose. We drank milk by the quart. The source of these luxuries was of course the small cheques which still arrived from the wholesale newsagents. Paid over to our printer they would have made no immediate impression on the debt we owed him, and we suspended these payments, letting the small liquid reserve accumulate as the stake out of which he, and we ourselves, would win back a sounder sum from the new hazard. Our minds were in no way burdened with thought of the future. We were preparing for it as thoroughly as we were able, and the present seemed to glow quite brightly by the stimulation of our fed and fit senses.

Now we fell in with a stroke of luck—the first fortunate coincidence which had come our way for a twelvemonth. About the end of our second week at the gymnasium there arrived a man whom Charlie described casually as a ship's officer. He was heavily built, appeared to us to be somewhere in his thirties, and he was apparently an intermittent pupil during his spells ashore. From the start he buckled into his tasks with red-faced grimness, knowing the suffering that lay ahead. In a voice accustomed to command, but softened somewhat by present agony, he would, from out of his writhing, coax Charlie, in vain, to shorten the separate ordeals. Heavy-limbed, he found the leg-waving a bitter task, and once jerked out the appeal: 'Have a heart, Charlie!' 'Hert?' exclaimed Charlie, with the air of a man whose kindly nature constantly defeats his judgment. 'It's a' hert thegether!'

It was soon evident that all this was preparation for a nobler art. In a day or two there arrived, by arrangement, a companion for our fellow-pupil in the squat shape of a sparring partner. The newcomer had a gentle disposition out of character with his corpse-like skin and crumpled ears of the professional boxer. The two of them donned gloves as big as marking buoys and pounded each other doggedly in a manner to rock the building. We were entranced by this authentic demonstration of toughness, and in the following days allowed our imaginations to place the seaman in the rôle of bucko mate, preparing to embark on a voyage round the Horn, with a rough and salty crew capable of being disciplined only by the strong arm.

We were, fortunately, wrong. Captain Campbell, shortly to achieve his present status as one of the famous Clyde river pilots, was at that time navigating officer in the West Coast of Scotland fishery cruiser. Here was, brought together with us under that Spartan roof in Edinburgh, probably one of the best living authorities in the seafaring problems of the chancy Hebridean seas. He knew that coast as intimately as he knew the planks and cracks of Charlie Cotter's floor. We could have consulted a hundred fisher and coastal vessel men, friends of our own, learning from them of the sheltered bays and tricks of the tide that lay all along the orthodox routes. But Campbell had for years taken a sizable craft constantly off the usual tracks, using hides and anchorages that were not even charted, to find and intercept the poachers of the sea fishings. He knew how the waters ran in every creek and off every headland, and what they did with the wind in each airt. Gathered up within him was the knowledge that might have been shared by the dozen best smugglers of the seventeen-nineties, but which had not likely been before in the possession of one man.

His knowledge was a treasure to us, and we grilled him for it daily after the shower. At night we worked over the charts we were to take, marking the white sheets with Campbell wisdom. When climbing, or sailing, one is always cautioned to seek local advice and information. These are gladly given, and are misleading with shaking frequency. On our trip, where local knowledge conflicted with what Campbell had told us, we always found that Campbell was right. He was, in addition, one of the only orthodox seamen we encountered before the trip who did not dismiss the affair as an adolescent escapade, and too dangerous to succeed. But then a master mariner, and a Campbell at that, who spends his shore leave in paying a professional boxer to punch him hurtfully, no doubt learns to be careful about which forms of juvenile folly he condemns.

The time had come to get our seafaring equipment in order. Over in Queensferry the canoes were almost ready. We bought charts covering the Clyde to the farthest Hebrides. I have mentioned their white sheets, although they came back from the voyage with us sodden to a tattered limpness, stained with salt and sweat, and ribboned here and there into veteran strips as a result of urgent consultation on seas which were violent and wet. Such traces of usage follow when the chart tables of an expedition —our knees—are mostly under water.

We pooled our existing climbing and camping gear, to discover that over the past year most of it had been in use, to comfort our sojourn in the *Claymore* office. Somebody lent us a tent, a splendid sturdy square little creation six feet high with twelve-inch walls and a central pole. I wonder at what age people like ourselves cease to have more affection for a tent than for a house. This one was greatly loved by us from the start, although we did not know then how often in the next three months its cloth walls would stand like a rampart between us and our discomforts and doubts. It was a tent whose interior knew more hopeful joy than most houses.

Only a few essential items remained to purchase, and we thought we could see a way to do this without the rash expenditure of money. Many of our advertisers had been firms catering for the outdoors market, and they had wisely seen in the *Claymore* the ideal medium to put them in touch with a new and youthful public eager for camping accessories. There was a Glasgow firm whose proprietor had driven a very hard bargain with Seumas in the matter of space-rates. Moreover, his bill for the last series of insertions was not yet paid, and, knowing our man, we guessed that it would remain so as soon as he discovered the paper to be no longer a going concern. We felt it only right that one of our advertisers should get our personal business, particularly as we had no intention of paying for the articles. We hastened to his premises, happily outdistancing the news that our journal was defunct. Attended by the proprietor himself, we were supplied and carefully fitted with a wind- and waterproof jerkin apiece, a couple of paraffin pressure stoves, and some light-weight cooking utensils, to a total almost equal to his debt to us. 'Send the bill', we said, bearing off our parcels, while the proprietor bowed us out as one business man to two others. It was clear the hint had not reached him that we had abandoned this rôle.

At another shop, also our debtors for recent advertising, we fared in a softer-hearted manner. When we got there to place our modest pro-rata orders, we found the concern about to close down, and in the first stages of selling-off the entire shop stock at throwaway bargain prices. Failures were in the air, it seemed, that summer. We came away, by choice, empty-handed.

It was the 15th of August. Word came from John Marshall that the canoes were finished and had been sent to us by rail.

CHAPTER III

THE START

With the Skerries for my milestones, and the sun's salute, and rain—
Send my heart by Kishmul's Galley and my body by MacBrayne.
When I'm old I'll take the steamer, but the first boat was my ain.

THE canoes which John Marshall had made for us were of a canvas-and-rubber fabric stretched over a tough teak framework, and were shaped in section like a slim spearhead. The pointed ends, separately made and sealed to form buoyancy tanks, were detachable. They were decked with highly varnished light wood, while the centre section, about six feet long, had a canvas deck laced loosely all round the top of the sides and by no means watertight. An ingenious safety measure was the incorporation into the deck structure of an inflated motor inner tube, into which we sat as in a cockpit. This gave a comfortable back-rest and, in an emergency, a lifebelt which could be snatched at a jerk out of its fitting. A waterproof apron studded by fasteners into the canvas of the deck stretched round our waists so that, *en voyage*, we appeared to be wearing the canoes like snug garments.

When assembled, the three sections—centre-piece and two points—were bound by a heavy and (we believed) unbreakable wire which ran from a bulkhead in front of the cockpit, passed in a groove over the bow point, along the keel beneath, came up over the stern, and was hooked to the cockpit bulkhead at the back. Each bulkhead fastening included a screw shackle which tightened the wire to a solid twanging strain, and the whole affair was held thus rigidly together. The length overall was thirteen and a half feet, and thirty-two inches in the beam. From deck to keel the measure was only twelve inches. The craft drew five or six inches of this when loaded, so that there remained about six inches of freeboard. Along the bottom of all three sections, protecting the fabric from the worst friction of shingled beach and rocks, ran a few narrow strips of wood. The weight assembled was about eighty pounds unloaded. The oar was a two-bladed paddle, dipped on either side alternately.

John Marshall had experimented with a mast and sails on some of these craft, and had found that with a small square sail he got very stimulating results on a following wind. We decided on some such installation, and looked forward to many happy hours of lolling at ease against our inflated back-rests, while the prevailing south-westerly wind bore us northwards during the sunny August days.

It was readily assumed by all who learned of our project that we had, over the years, accumulated the necessary range of experience in the handling of these precarious craft. 'Both are, of course, expert canoeists', was a phrase frequently appearing about this time in the preliminary paragraphs which we urged into print at the hands of kindly Glasgow journalists. The facts were somewhat otherwise. We had never even seen canoes at close quarters until a few weeks previously, and our only experience of handling them had been on a recent Sunday afternoon on the Forth and Clyde Canal, with an evening wallow across the upper Firth of Forth as our salt-water introduction to open seafaring. I had never at any time been under sail in an orthodox way, but Seumas had once spent a week in somebody's yacht in the Kyles of Bute. On the credit side was an intimate acquaintance from boyhood with rowing boats, on such mad terms of familiarity that we had frequently hoisted tents to serve as sails in a favourable wind. And we both, of course, knew very well the uncertain waters of the West Coast and the Hebrides, although this was a knowledge from which confidence in our prospects by no means followed.

The canoes were installed in the back garden of my parents' home in Westerton, Glasgow. We assembled our kit and experimented with all the varieties of bundling we could think of. Old rubber groundsheets were cut for packing materials, as we foresaw, with sinister accuracy, that our sleeping-bags and clothes might from time to time be under water. Two five-foot broomsticks were stepped as masts, and we made yard-square sails of light cloth, on bamboo spreaders (the latter from the chrysanthemums), with a cord arrangement which could raise and lower them from the cockpits like small cinematograph screens.

THE START 17

We had decided to start from the Clyde at Broomielaw, in the heart of Glasgow. I called upon Captain Eaglesham, the Clyde Trust's Harbourmaster, laying the scheme before him as one seafarer to another. He was amused, and even helpful, but not to be moved. It seems that, in a shipping river, vessels proceed only by special pilot licence, and it would have been embarrassing on both sides to inquire into our qualifications. He admitted, however, that his jurisdiction ended at Bowling, half-way down river to the Tail of the Bank, and it was to this place that our starting-point was switched. A great gathering of citizens would undoubtedly have been present at the Broomielaw to watch the setting forth, and the public enthusiasm so aroused would have been useful background publicity in the market of newspaper articles. At the time, we grudged sorely the loss of these few city miles. We needed a public, and we needed it quickly, if our writing was to make the vivid, adventurous and yet serious impression we wanted it to make.

It was obvious that the newspaper to which we could best attach ourselves for the supply of the voyage's descriptive articles was the *Daily Record*, which proudly called itself Scotland's National Newspaper, and meant it. Among the popular papers then and since it had the best-developed social conscience on Scots affairs. It was vigilant in the country's welfare, and while predominantly the paper of the industrial West, had a knowledgeable eye on the rural areas where four out of every five Scots town dwellers have their roots. We felt that the appearance of our articles in the *Daily Record* would suit our plans best, and we set about persuading the paper to think the same of us.

Most of the day before our departure date we spent in the *Daily Record* office, where we have since had a much closer association. The Editor agreed to look with sympathy on what we might send, although there was to be no guarantee of publication. This was probably the most that we could expect. Our story was, on the face of it, but a seasonal adventure, and only as it developed in scale could we compel a serious audience to note any of the thoughtful lessons we felt might be told after we had accumulated some freakish authority.

That the adventure might not develop very far was made plain when Mr. John Conn, Editor of the *Evening News*, another paper of the group, arrived at the conference we were having with some of the journalists of the morning paper. 'Have they been photographed?' he inquired. 'You know, in case . . .' and he turned to us, smiling with heavy reassurance. 'Not that we want anything to happen . . . but—you never know.' Weighing once more the elements of what makes news, we were conducted to the studio and photographed for, doubtless, some ultimately macabre purpose. The print went into the file, whence I removed it myself a short time ago. It records, upon our faces, the End of Youth.

Late that night we were still in the garden, putting the last touches to our ocean-going craft. Jim MacDougall, Robbie MacLean and John Burt, who had borne with us, in their spare time, the main burden of the *Claymore*'s production, came to help with the final stages of equipping the expedition. Until long after the daylight failed we worked by the light of candles stuck by their own grease on the taut canvas of the canoe decks. The night was still and windless, and the straight flames stood, in happy augury of calms to come, rigid four-inch lengths of illumination. This was to be the last spell for the next ten weeks when a candle would burn motionless in the open.

After midnight, when the tasks appeared finished and the other two had gone home, Jim decided to construct a tiny breakwater on the deck section of each canoe bow. This was a plywood V, pointing forward and a few inches high, which, Jim explained, would help to part the solid water we might ship over the bows. He fixed them to the decks with surgical elastic tape, and they hung on there until the end, staggering and tattered. They were never greatly useful, but we left them even after we knew better, as evidence of the pre-excursion anxieties of a man who knew much more about small craft than we did.

Something will have to be done about the education of the mothers of would-be explorers. Readers of J. M. Barrie will recall this topic as one which frequently preoccupied Margaret Ogilvie. It was necessary for us during these last hours of back-garden activity to be overheard quipping and jesting lightheartedly, in a manner which would appear to dismiss the project as a short-term and harmless romp. Early in the next afternoon a motor-lorry came to transport us and the canoes to Bowling. With Robbie and John to help, we carried the canoes singly out to the gate, taking care to cant them beamwise on the way down the path, so that my mother, watching from a window, should not be reminded of their undoubted structural resemblance to coffins. This ruse and its accompanying frolic in no way deceived that Highland imagination.

The four of us, kilted and windswept, stood astraddle of the canoes in the rear of the lorry as it hammered down to Bowling. We attracted a good deal of attention among the promenaders on the Knightswood Boulevard and along the Clyde waterfront, so that when we de-lorried ourselves and the canoes at Bowling, stumbling across the railway levels with the grossly weighted craft, an eager Saturday afternoon crowd surged on our heels. They had been waiting for us. It was a triumph of last-minute publicity, for Seumas had been able to find a couple of spare hours on the previous day to write a full-length preliminary article on the reasons for the trip, and it had appeared that morning in ample time to afford us a rendezvous with our public. They were present in large numbers, and since that woebegone picture had also been used to illustrate the tale, the fingers and voices of recognition were raised on all sides.

It would be true to say that the article had struck a challenging note. Starting with a stage-by-stage detail of our route—Firth of Clyde; Kyles of Bute; Loch Fyne; Crinan Canal; the Dorus Mor; Seil Sound; Firth of Lorne; Oban; Sound of Mull; Ardnamurchan Point; the Small Isles of Eigg, Rhum, and Muck; Mallaig; Sound of Sleat; Skye; the Minch; Harris; Stornoway —it went on:

'We shall meet with criticism. We have met it already. Canoeing, we are told, isn't feasible in Scottish waters, and to take a canoe up the Hebrides is foolhardy.

'With armchair critics we have no common ground. To others we would say this: From our earliest days as a people we have been building and sailing boats. We are a maritime race in the completest sense. But intensive industrialisation has lost us our contact with the sea. Steamers have made us forget the thrills of small-craft sailing. We want to taste the zest of physical living that town life denies us.

'But there is something more. After the sailing comes the seeing. We want to see the Western Isles thoroughly, to complete our own picture of them. Not the Isles of the guide-books, but the real isles—the Isles of Opportunity, peopled by a vigorous race with an unrivalled climate for some types of products; islands capable of supporting more of our surplus population in large-sized holdings yielding an adequate return.

'Therein is our real adventure—exploring the possibilities for expansion and development in our own country.'

Something of this novel and possibly naïve challenge had already, it seemed, conveyed itself to the people who came to see our start. The only itinerant writing about the Scottish rural scene up to that time had depicted the countryside as a bracing background to physical adventure, but playing no significant part in the story. What Seumas had been saying in his incautious preliminary was that it was the land and the people, and not we, which would make our story. They would take the foreground, and we would try to make ourselves a part of that scene and life. It seemed to augur well that already so many people appeared to see our point.

The negative note, however, was also being resoundingly struck. 'You'll never come back. We've seen the last of you!' was the hearty farewell greeting of a Stornoway friend. And one of the harbour men, impelled to offer a professional opinion, used for the first time the phrase that was to run like a yellow thread of defeat through the whole dark and plaided pattern of our voyage: 'It's too late in the year!'

There was a gratifying attendance of reporters and photographers, for whom we spoke or postured on demand. The portability of the canoes had captured the public fancy, and it was proposed that we should be photographed in a manner to illustrate this, each man standing on the stone-edged beach with his canoe under his arm. Loaded as they were with kit and comforts, the canoes by their sheer weight made this a manifest impossibility. The four of us, however, hoisted one canoe, and then Robbie and John leapt backwards out of the camera's eye, leaving 'the two daring canoeists', with wan smiles, straining to hold the thing waist-high. Our arms gave out as the snapshotting finished, and the load fell heavily to the beach.

At last we got aboard, stuffing our kilts down the sides of the cockpits like shirts into trousers. Robbie and John launched us away, walking fully clad knee-high into the water to set our laden bulk afloat. The crowd delighted in this hardy gesture, and we departed basking for a moment in the reflected credit. If those left behind—so ran the public thought—could treat the sea with such nonchalance, the principals of the expedition must be robust indeed. Fresh photographs recorded the chilly scene. Then we drove at the awkward paddles to a thin dribble of cheering, lurching round the pier into the river. Peter Leddy, the Alexandria photographer, shouted from his perch on a bollard: 'Wave!'—and our hands were raised obediently to his lens. 'Waving a cheery farewell', was the lying caption which carried this scene in Monday's papers. A few more uncertain strokes took us clear of Bowling Harbour.

It was a grey day, with a westerly wind in our faces up-river, and a short wet chop splashing over the low bows. But in twenty minutes of paddling we had the feel of the canoes, moving with them, the wobble created by our over-anxious thighs gone for ever. We held to the north side of the river, between the main channel and the shore, and shortly stroked our way past the rotting piles of Dumbarton's old pier, where the Clyde opens out towards the Firth. There was a little outward-bound shipping in the channel south of us. Although our progress was slow enough, our arms were not tiring, the push-pull leverage of the paddling being well within our new powers. From the first we were ceaselessly conscious of the wind, an awareness which was to last and grow until the trip was done. Opposite Port Glasgow it seemed to have backed well to the south; we felt that the time had come to hoist sail. And so we did, the scraps of canvas filling out splendidly in the beam wind. In no time at all we were rattling ashore among the reeds of the Cardross shallows. It was the quickest method of learning that only a stern wind will travel a sailing canoe. With sails stowed, we scraped off again and slapped a damp passage round the point of Ardmore into Craigendoran Bay. By this time we knew of a pervading wetness about our persons. Several baling pauses removed a substantial body of water from about our limbs, while spray from the little bursting rollers drove at us like a ceaseless heavy rain.

With the broadening of the river towards Greenock and the Firth we felt for the first time another of the sensations familiar to sailors—the dwindling support of the shore and the wide spaciousness of waters. South to the sea the scene was bleak and cold. For that night, however, we had a heartening prospect —a camp with the three others among the firs on Rosneath Point. We had arranged a meeting with them in the water off Helensburgh.

Splashing ahead, and now tiring, we paddled down on to a rowing-boat which contained Robbie and John. They had squelched out of the water at Bowling Harbour, taken a bus to Helensburgh, dried their feet at a tearoom fire somewhere, and put off to meet us in a hired boat. They greeted our bedraggled arrival with taciturn relief. At least we were still afloat, if wallowing, and we had come ten miles. The old *Lucy Ashton*, her paddles hammering, passed on her last run for the night, stirring up an extra surge about us. Passengers, with the impassivity of the steamer-borne, leaned on the rails to see us. A mile off, between us and the Rosneath shore, a speck showed Jim in his own eleven-foot canoe. As we came up to him he raised a paddle in an antique salute, and we were all soon in the sheltered water below our camp ground. When the canoes grounded, Seumas and I, kilted and cramped, flopped from the cockpits like sodden dishclouts out of a sink.

The next hour we spent in cutting down our equipment by half. At least we were learning quickly, and it was already clear that we had no possible expectation of travelling dry. Any sort of sea would constantly search its way through the deck lacing, while we were to know many an occasion when it would break solidly into the cockpit itself. All the extras went into a heap— tweed jackets, a rug, most of the spare clothes and luxuries. The constant threat of the rising weather among the pine-tops spurred our assessment of impediments, and we stripped ourselves to the limit in an austere new burst of simplicity.

The camp was pitched then, well inland from the shore. It was to be the last time the five of us would camp together. We had for a dozen years camped and lived together, or in twos or threes of that five, in every part of Scotland and the islands. In this company we had, it seemed, grown up more in our tents than in our own homes. And if we are ever together again, time and tide will have stopped running.

CHAPTER IV

JOURNEY WITH A MELON

> Let the end come, if it will,
> In some dour place apart—
> Not at the foot of the hill,
> Not in sight of the start.

PACKING was a lighter task the next morning. Robbie and John loaded the bundle of our discarded equipment into their boat, for the delivery of these effects to our homes. The wind was higher from the south-west, driving sizable waves on to our shore. By early afternoon, when a start could no longer be delayed, it had not slackened. Dressed this time only in singlets, shorts, and jerkins, we got off by lifting the canoe bows high into about two feet of water, standing with one foot in the bottom of the cockpit, and pushing with the other on the shingle as if propelling a scooter. Later we became very expert at this. The trick is to keep the bows high so that they do not pierce the oncoming waves and so allow the gaping cockpit to gulp a mouthful. Eventually our small flotilla was drawing a wet course into the wind along the shore towards Kilcreggan at the entrance to Loch Long.

Canoes are never happy in the short steep waves of firth water, but we took this weather much better than the rowing-boat. Robbie and John were getting it very wet in bursts over their bow, and soon they decided, for their time was up anyway, to turn and run back for Helensburgh. We shouted an inarticulate farewell back and forth, watching them for a few seconds enviously as they stroked expertly downwind out of sight behind us. Jim, still anxious to try another trim in the disposal of our gear, paddled on with us for a mile or two until we went ashore with him on a small beach beyond Portkil.

He fussed with us there for a few minutes, in a manner which betrayed, as he admitted later, that he did not expect to see us again. He said 'Watch yourselves', and again 'Watch yourselves', and looking vaguely down the south horizon towards Arran: 'Don't be afraid to give it up'. Then he shook hands with us brusquely—a gesture rarely resorted to among us—and got into his own cockpit. We waded in with his canoe held sideways like a stretcher, and launched him vigorously beyond the backwash. He was good with boats of all kinds, and knew more about canoes than any of us, having led our *Claymore* Hebridean expedition. A few paddle strokes put him in position to exploit the wind. Up went his rag of sail, like a half balloon, and with his bamboo mast whipping in an archer's bow he was swept away from us round Portkil Point. 'On our own now' is how the log records this moment.

A few Sunday afternoon strollers had by this time arrived on the beach, and took up stances to watch the experts put to sea. We scootered off the shore with indifferent skill. My open cockpit swallowed a solid wave-top, so that I crammed in at last to sit down in a rocking douche speckled with seaweed. Seumas had quit the shore more cannily, but was flung broadside by a comber and came bumping in again. By the time I could turn round to watch him he was completely aground lengthways, high but far from dry, and getting every wave over him as it hammered and exploded on the canoe's flank. While his inshore paddle scraped the shingle ridiculously, seeking an oarful of water on the land, a splendid lassie ran down from the group of spectators, stripped off her shoes and stockings in a motion, and pushed him off, wading out with him until he was clear. I joined Seumas's abashed and chagrined courtesies, and the two of us then bent to a face-saving violence of paddling until we got out of sight towards Kilcreggan.

We camped that night in the back garden of our old friend John L. Kinloch at Kilcreggan. This bearded Greenock dominie had already taken a boyish delight in our *Claymore* efforts. The canoe trip was precisely the kind of seriously-intentioned escapade which he understood. His school-teaching career had been milestoned with a series of exuberant outbursts, big with prestige and Scottish patriotism, including the formation, at the time of the Barra land raids, of a triumphant Highland Land League on a capital of thirty shillings. It was good to meet him at this brooding initial stage of the trip. The next few days, whatever

1. THE START. *To show the canoes' portability, the photographers wanted each man to pose with his canoe under his arm. We just managed to hold up one between us, dropping it as soon as this snapshot was taken. Seumas stands on the left.*

2. DEPARTURE FROM BOWLING. *Robbie MacLean, also up to his knees in water, took this picture of John Burt getting ready to push us off.*

3. OUR FIRST NIGHT OUT. *The kilted figure in the centre of the camp at Rosneath is Jim MacDougall.*

the weather, would mean a slog of paddling among the waterside suburbs of Glasgow which had little meaning for our story. Not until we were in Loch Fyne, or even beyond the Crinan Canal, would we reach the Highlands and the mere beginning of the journey's significance. Yet it would be easy to meet disaster in the Firth of Clyde, in this weather which was now driving a cold body of sea upon the shore and scourging our world with lashings of rain.

After a heartening meal we strolled a mile into Cove village, where I had passed much of my boyhood, to pay respects to my old Aunt Kate and Aunt Mary Gordon. No one that I remember ever left their home without bearing a bouquet of flowers from their old-fashioned garden, but Aunt Mary recognised that such trophies would ill match our voyaging, and searched for some time in her cupboard after a more practical donative. We came away bearing a superb melon, as obviously the largest and most detachable section of her kindly store, and the most manageable addition to ours. The homeward mile was beguiled by rugby passing the melon from hand to hand across the breadth of the road.

That melon brought our packing problem to a head at once. It enabled us to simplify in a single session our whole future technique of kit stowage. Every morning thereafter when we struck camp each man packed into his canoe his own personal gear and such common chattels as he could lay hands on. As the stuff disappeared in an atmosphere of wary haste, the time would come when one of us would announce levelly: 'I'm full', and proceed to lace up his deck, leaving the laggard to find space for the odd items—indeed helping him to cram them in. This method imposed a discipline of speed upon the expedition. It was purely the invention of Seumas, who first made the announcement in an understandable mood of self-defence, some time about midday on the drenched Kilcreggan beach. We had both avoided the melon. Into my own craft I stuffed the other extra things, and even then the exotic item lay unclaimed. I lobbed it into my cockpit, bitterly aware that I must shortly joust with it for hip-room, and we set to the slippery task of launching.

The tide was far out, with the low-water rocks large and weed-covered. The Rosneath constable, slanting into the wind as he cycled along the empty road on his way to Cove, was hailed by

John Kinloch to our aid, and the four of us floundered with the canoes in two trips to the uproar at the tide's edge. Canoes out of water are, like seals, awkward in transit. But we got afloat and pushed off quickly through the inshore disturbance, myself wriggling to a sitting posture like a nesting bird, in conflict with the melon. The wind, filled with solid rain, was still stiff from the south-west, and our route was straight into its eye down the Firth of Clyde. As our first goal we headed for Dunoon, a four-mile passage which would be our longest open-water jump so far. There we could expect the shelter of a weather shore for most of the way down to Toward Point. This stretch was a very hard pull of an hour and a half, but we were now weathering well, and no longer flinching before the solid thrown wave-tops which struck our faces. Ahead at intervals we could see the black ruffle of heavier squalls coming down on us, to hold us stopped, forcing a harder stroke from us even to stand still. In the more open part of the Firth, although the weather did not rest, we delighted in the longer and higher waves over which we could ride the canoes dry and comfortably. A six-metre yacht, gloriously handled by a solitary man in yellow oilskins, came up on the wind like a pillar of spray, with hard-filled jib and mainsail, running for the Gare Loch. We shouted a greeting or two as he drove past a few yards away, a swan dwarfing two water-beetles.

By the time we reached the lee of the land off Dunoon the slashing rain had dwindled to a drizzle, and we could raise our heads from the flog of wind and water. At this stage Seumas sportingly agreed to take over the melon, which had been resting like a gross wen upon my right thigh. Crowds of people gathered thickly along the promenade railings, as if awaiting some grand event seawards, and in a moment it became clear from their shouts of welcome that they were waiting for us. We had already become celebrities. Recognising the obligations of this rôle, Seumas gave the crowd of a thousand or more its money's worth by paddling inshore below the statue of Highland Mary and baling out his canoe. It was a gratifying sight for all as he hitched himself up in the cockpit repeatedly and flung canfuls of water back where it had come from. This was carried out with a flair, although he was having a running fight below decks with the melon. Every time he raised his hips to get at the plentiful sea-water the melon would roll below him, and have to be bowled back. In the end, during one of these conflicts, he sat on it heavily. I heard the squash from twenty waves away. It was now disc-shaped, but immobile, as he stuffed it behind him and flourished on with his pannikin to the plaudits of Scotland on holiday. Cheers of genuine appreciation were rising.

When we paddled on along the shore the crowds moved, following us, and the younger among them ran ahead to hire rowing-boats and share with us the now ennobled waters of the bay. I confess we were pleased about this. It seemed to announce an encouraging understanding of what we were up to. Also it emphasised again the value of that first *Daily Record* story, and what we could do with well-timed reports, if we could get them published. The Sunday papers had described our departure scenes at Bowling, inaccurately but at length, and a little farther without mishap would bring us to the real action phase of our story-telling.

At the far end of Dunoon Bay we had a mighty reception from the boys of the Orphan Homes of Scotland, as they played bare-legged on the sand below their holiday camp. There was repeated three-cheering, and when a treble voice shrilled above the rest 'Come in here, mister!' we turned inshore. They lifted their small breeks to a man and splashed out towards us, leaving their teachers on the edge of the surf. We floated low in a foot of water, with the smallest of them towering above us—chattering, bursting with delight, patting the canoes:

'Are you going to the New Hebrides?'

'We've been watching for you.'

'We read about it in the papers.'

It was some time before we left them, for they were of an age to keep, longer than adults, the taste of second-hand adventure. They cheered us in a receding chorus, a hundred eager bairns, not one with a mother or a father to his name.

The next stage was a straight paddle down the eight-mile stretch of shore to Toward Point. We dipped and swung into this in good style, the motion now coming easily. Holding well in to the shore, we were on a middle course between the comfortable cars which passed on the road a hundred yards to our right, and the passenger steamers of these well-served waters a hundred yards to our left. Rowing-boats stood off the shore so that their occupants could stare at oar's-length. There is, unfortunately, none of the casual exchange of greetings among seafaring passers-by to which one is accustomed in hill and moor encounters, and few of these onlookers spoke to us directly, although there was a good deal of nautical muttering in every boatload as we passed. So we progressed on the flank of the steamer track which leads to Rothesay, past Innellan, and down towards Toward Lighthouse, where the wind hit us again suddenly. It was throwing a formidable sea upon the Point and into our teeth. For the first few minutes of it we made almost no headway at all, although paddling in an effort that tore at our chests, while the broken inshore water lapped over and into us and the waves on our weather side punched us off our line.

In the long half-hour fight that took place among the rocky backwash on the Point we learned a good deal about canoeing and the individual malice of waves. At this time we knew nothing at all about how to deal with breakers, but our apprenticeship was now well begun. Emerging beyond Toward Point red-eyed and sitting in three inches of water, we turned to the right westwards for the Kyles of Bute, where we had hoped to camp for the night. An early dusk was coming, and the rain with it. After a few hundred yards farther, with heavy but now regular waves on our beam, we decided to turn in to land and find a camp site on Toward. It meant another landing on a lee shore. Fortunately we struck a sand beach, towards which we went rolling very sweetly with the stern seas running under us. This time we had an idea of what should be done. As the bows touched we were overboard running the canoes up the sand before the next wave could hit the stern and fill the vacant cockpit.

The tent sprang up like a peaked mushroom beside a fence which bordered farm fields running inland. The two stoves roaring inside dried the sodden grass and our stripped selves. On the spread groundsheets we then pulled into our sleeping-bags and, lying on our elbows, cooked and ate the historic Toward Banquet, which consisted of pease brose, oatmeal brose, the melon, stew, canned fruit, a loaf and a half, a pot of jam, cheese, oatcakes, oranges, and lashings of tea. In the intervals between courses we lifted the storm-bulged door-flap to watch the lights and neon signs of Rothesay three and a half miles away across the water. Out of the black sky above the town, which delights in calling itself 'The Madeira of Scotland', the best part of a full gale was punishing the Firth.

The tent stood up to it well during the night, although Seumas was out twice double-pegging the ropes and walls. By the morning the wind had blown itself out, leaving only a dreary rain absently falling. With sodden kilts buckled on again, to play a shore rôle, we took the bus to Dunoon. There we tramped incognito the rain-blashed streets which yesterday our arrival had emptied seawards. Our search was for some truly reliable packing material to contain our gear, as it was clearly doomed for the rest of the trip to be awash during the daylight hours. The rubber and oilskin swathings of the present arrangement had by a treacherous combination of condensation and leaking delivered up our clothes and sleeping-bags in a progressively damp state over the past days. And heavens! we had hardly reached Rothesay, which is about as far into the Highlands as Maryhill.

A knowing girl in a back-street draper's shop produced the right thing without a trace of fuss—American oilcloth, which we had hitherto seen only as a covering for kitchen tables. We bore away a roll of this stuff, leaving behind a great deal of money by current standards, and from that moment our packing troubles were done with.

A call on the kindly Mr. and Mrs. Lowe at Toward Point Farm also solved our accommodation problem for the same night. When darkness fell, and the skies with it, we were in an empty hayloft festooned at all points with raftered sleeping-bags, groundsheets, tent, canvas decks, and every garment we owned. Cooking the evening meal was a spacious affair after the crowded quarters of the tent. Later, with a tea-box for a table and two candles going, we wrote up our logs portentously—but never a word for the newspapers. They would hear from us when we got to the Highlands, and the sooner the better.

At last the next morning was almost fair, and improving, with the sun coming as we heaved all the stuff back to the beach again. Two girls and two lads in their teens scampering on the sand before bathing were the first to benefit from our determined policy of sharing our ploy with the local people wherever we might be. Some of our happiest hours came from the times we spent giving practice trips to anybody who asked for them.

Hundreds throughout the West will remember their first rocky paddlings in our canoes. These youngsters on Toward Beach were the first, and they made some delighted circuits of the bay.

Then we got away. This was an easy day, with a little northerly wind which dwindled through the Kyles of Bute until, when we camped near Tighnabruaich, it was in the midst of a calm and midge-infested evening. Joy followed in the morning with a north-west wind at our backs down the second leg of the Kyles. With our absurd sails set like galleys on souvenir brooches, we drew off among the distinguished yachts crowding the bay. Many of them enjoyed a much closer look than we had intended, for the full spread of our canvas obliterated our view forward, and the only method by which we could see ahead while sailing was to lean forward and lift the bottom of the sail temporarily like a window-blind—a far from nautical manoeuvre. We had by this time, however, assumed a noticeable nonchalance, and found time to offer passing greetings to the largely unresponsive yachtsmen as we scraped a way through. The more boat-proud among them made unnecessary moves towards fenders and boat-hooks, although they were in considerably less peril than we. These scenes of superior life afloat were soon left behind.

It was a delightful run down the Kyles, with only intermittent paddle strokes urging the canoes on. This wind, taking us along busily, promised trouble when we got to Ardlamont Point and turned north into Loch Fyne, but that was still miles and hours away. It died occasionally, and then built up with more force. By the time we were abreast of Blair's Ferry we were happy in our proved sailing asset, and we went ashore for a time to celebrate by cooking a considerable lunch. It was a luxury we were not again to permit ourselves. We never again had a cooked meal in the middle of a travelling day.

And so on to Ardlamont Point in the afternoon, with the wind strengthening behind us. The sun went, leaving the day gurly. A sea was travelling with us, hoisting the stern points and running alongside at deck level until the passing waves escaped out from below our bows. The island of Bute fell away east to our left, and the view ahead was immense, with Arran a huge and remote mass, which might have been ten times the seven miles our splashed chart told us was the distance. Inch Marnock huddled under a drive of spray and rain belching from the black heart of Loch Fyne, whose entrance we could now see opening inwards from Skipness. Mile-wide dark waves with their tops bursting were galloping out of the loch and fighting with our own Kyles sea on Ardlamont's shoals. Near the Point a black buoy span and bowed, its clear flash a reminder of the diminishing daylight.

Hereabouts, as the land on our right dropped lower to the Point, billows of wind poured over from the west and met in conflict with our steady stern breeze, so that squalls and swirls hit us and we zigzagged, but still onwards. On one of these blasts I drove a sudden course off-shore, and 'Mind that buoy!' shouted Seumas. 'I'm watching it'—I heaved at the stiffened sail in the hope of a forward view, but couldn't raise it for a moment against the pressure of wind that kept it spread and straining. 'Right! Paddle right!' came from Seumas, and I scooped three heaving oarfuls on the right. Then the buoy blotted out my shoreward vision, too quick to get my paddle inboard. The blade gonged the metal tank like a knell, with Seumas laughing along his wiser-chosen course on the other side.

We got our sails down as the Point came abreast, paddling in to make a landing. From the higher level of the shore there was little comfort in the sight of Loch Fyne. The last run down the wind had left us reluctant to face a wet pull into it, although our decided goal for the night was Tarbert, or at least that side of the loch. We unshipped our masts, stowing them and the sails below decks to give us the least wind resistance. Later against headwinds we always travelled mastless, and learned even to crouch like T.T. riders going upwind. In this way we sneaked a kindergarten passage round the Point and for three miles up the Loch Fyne shore, where, except for one or two half-exposed beaches, we had shelter and were rarely in more than four feet of water. The Skate Islands were to be our jumping-off for the wallow across the loch, and until we reached the first of them this contour voyaging, as in a paddling pool, kept our thoughts away from the noisy malevolence on our left. In this easy way we came up to the Wee Skate, startling a long dormitory of resting seals so that they dived simultaneously like a breaking wave. Landing on their ledge, we tethered the canoes by their lifted bows run up on the rocks, and stood there for a time, whistling through mouths full of bread to coax the seals up. Some of them surfaced, more worried than charmed, and blew rudely through their whiskers.

The first stage was simple, to the Big Skate with its winking beacon. Beyond this shelter we got it badly. It was on Loch Fyne we learned to like beam seas. They came down on our right high and quickly, but clean. In maybe half an hour of splashing and misjudgment we had the trick of the haunch roll that lifted us flat on to the waves and seemed to twitch them onwards under us and away. The wind, we found, was our real enemy here, and not the increasing waves, for it kept us off the line we had made for Loch Tarbert, and we soon knew that our limit was to keep from losing ground downward and out of the loch towards Arran. Eventually we were able to hold a straight course across, pointing to the highest of the land ahead. This, if we remembered rightly, would take us to the bay marked on the chart as Fionn Phort. It was now too dark to read the chart. But this was enjoyable, and tiring only on our left arms, with the extra work they had in holding us up against the forcing of the wide wind. Other occupants of the loch also found that it was fun. Porpoises started to roll in the breakers, until, near us, with disconcerting zest, they set to leaping clear of the water like salmon, the grunts of their untidy descent sounding like sighs heaved over our inept progress. We hoped their underwater eyesight was good, and that fins were not revving up for a take-off under our keels. This uncomfortable company subsided after we were more than half-way across. We were exchanging pleasantries of well-schooled relief when, less than fifty yards from our bows, four of the brutes in line left the water, heaving in our direction like a charging three-quarter line, arched over in glistening mid-air unison, and struck the water together, leaving four rising fountains which only the next wave dispersed.

'Come closer!' we shouted to each other. But one of them overheard. We were not ten yards apart on a converging course when a black torpedo burst from the water between us. It was a beautiful movement, as we agreed—but later! We saw the whites of his piggy eyes, slewing (we swore) from one to the other of us; heard his horrid *pech* in mid-air; then he was in with a mighty splash and tail-flip and we were off on a terrific burst on the last mile shorewards. I was downwind, and got the spray of him. He was the last we saw, but he gave a great impetus to our final lap for the night.

It was quite dark inshore. Entering the shelter of Fionn Phort, we saw ahead the riding lights of boats. They were two Tarbert fishing skiffs which had taken refuge there, and as the canoes passed they were getting up anchor to make for the herring grounds in Kilbrennan Sound. From their deck level the men could probably just see our pointed outlines black against the dusky water. They knew about us, and scolded with the quick judgment of the professional in his own sphere. We were well inshore when their last hails came. One was inevitable: 'It's too late in the year.' And then, more novel: 'Ye should be put in jail for going to sea in boats like that!'

There was never a better camp in all our trip than the one we had in Fionn Phort. Above the steep shore a flat little plateau ran level to the cliff foot on the three shoreward sides. A burn leapt in waterfalls down the rock face and spread at last to the loch in a murmuring delta. It was a desirable spot, typical of the countless abandoned homestead sites of the West. But from the very edge of the grass, and choking the whole plateau, a jostling growth of giant bracken flourished, so thickly that we could not push a way in. With our knives we cut a path six feet forward, and started at that point to pull up the bracken fronds singly by the roots. Soon we had a little clearing in which we could turn round. It grew to two yards square, then three yards, and that was enough for us. On the sweet grass of this patch we pitched the tent, and the bracken rose a foot above its top. Wind eddies, spilling in from the loch, flogged the burnside bushes. Standing at the tent door with an arm upheld we could feel the gusts cold on our fingers. But in our snug clearing there was not a whisper. Something of a calm was on us too. We ate, and slept, and awoke in the Highlands.

CHAPTER V

THE KINSMAN

> Victim and shaper of the laws—
> The memories' rich wale of him
> Abide to show the man he was,
> Rather than my poor tale of him.

WITH the daylight the gale died, although we did not guess it at the time, cut off as we were in our thicket of bracken. Our awakening was a slow and soaring sweep upwards from limp depths, until the velvet warmth left our eyes and let them open, and the morning air was cold and bracing in our noses. The bracken stems squeaked thickly together in a dying wind. Their frondy tops, like palms in an oasis, stroked moving shadows on the tent top as the sun came up.

We lay luxuriating for a while, in the satisfaction of having fairly started. The preliminaries were over; the trip was begun; we had entered our course, and could now stand up and be seen; everything we met and saw from now onwards was valid to our purpose. In this mood, with only our heads emerging from our sleeping-bags, we shaped up some noble passages for a couple of articles which would be despatched from Tarbert later that day. Then, rising, we crashed through the bracken to the beach to greet a balmy morning. The long fiord of Loch Fyne stretched away from us with an innocent sparkle, as if conflict with its dark tumult could never involve us, and many another man before and after. We dipped our cans in the burn for morning tea and porridge, and soon we were thrusting out of the bay in well-fed urgency.

This elation bore us northwards towards the port of Tarbert. The few miles we had to travel took us along the foot of the steep-to rocks, amid a lazily dying swell. There was even a little heat in the sun. The smells of the sea and the land were in our noses at the same time, and three or four fathoms below, as we stopped often to tilt and peer at them, bushes of seaweeds waved in the currents, with fish fending among their stems. When Loch Tarbert opened out, and the first houses appeared, we dressed ship—a process completed by combing our hair and smoothing out our waterproof aprons with a housewifely gesture—and stroked a tidy course in unison up to the end of the landlocked harbour. Here we stepped out literally on to the main street, leaving the canoes half on the pavement and half in the sea. Fishermen and holiday-makers came crowding round, eager but courteously silent, although in the more distant parts of the town could be heard the hurrying cries of: 'The canoes! . . . Canoes . . .!'

Tarbert is a dramatic place, with its houses and churches stepping up the crags which cup it in. On one of the rockshelves is a castle which was known to Robert the Bruce, and the foreign trade in herrings is so ancient that Tarbert is probably one of the oldest centres in the United Kingdom in continuous production with the same commodity. The water of East Loch Tarbert, round which the town is built, searches in westwards among the houses and almost bites through the peninsula of Kintyre. The isthmus (or *tairbeart*, the Gaelic word) separating Tarbert from West Loch Tarbert, a branch of the Atlantic, is not much wider than a mile, and about the end of last century it was scheduled for linking by a canal.

At this time the local herring industry was enduring one of its periodic miseries. The capricious herring, which in these parts has been honoured by the association of its name with that of Loch Fyne, frequently fails to return the courtesy. From time to time the shoals disappear entirely from the loch, and often from the entire coast. They had now been elusive for a period of years, and disaster was coming on the Loch Fyne fishing. One by one the little villages between Tarbert and Inveraray were dropping out of the ruin—Loch Gair, Minard, Furnace, Newton, Strachur. The older men and their small light skiffs had searched to the limit of their course, and now, crew by crew, were going to other jobs or the dole, and maintenance was failing on the boats. Had the young village men come into the business in these days they could well have sustained it until the herring returned. New boats, new energy, would have carried them fast and far, until the shoals had found their way inevitably back to the great water of their race.

But these middle nineteen-thirties were not a time of homing for men or fish. Such national leadership as existed pointed to the future with a shaking finger. The Highlander who might be disposed to look for future profit from his own resources was likely to be named a laughable figure of reaction. So they turned their backs upon the sea: took jobs as labourers and navvies, or set out again on the old emigrant quest, scourged by poverty round the world. The boats died on the shore and lay in dozens like animal skeletons. The negative façade behind which the Celt hides so much of his endeavour now came easily to his aid. 'The fishing's done' had become the commonest phrase of these shores. Of course, the fishing was not done. But the men were done.

Suddenly, out of nowhere, the shoals of herring came surging back up Loch Fyne. In the year or two before the war they teemed nightly in millions as far inland as Inveraray. From Fife, and Ayrshire, and farther afield, came the modern boats in hundreds, scooping up the treasure and turning it to gold. On the shore, straightening their backs from the stone-breaking at the quarries or the roadsides, the remnants of the best coastal fishermen and seamen in the world—boatless, netless, and grounded—watched them do it.

The full force of this change did not strike Tarbert. The vitality of a community larger than the hamlets kept them at the task and brought them to their later rewards. Their splendid fleet of boats is now a sight to see, and even the younger men tell me that the life and the living are comfortable. They have money and enjoy it—and why shouldn't they!—although the day's round of some of them brings cries of envious criticism from the old fishermen. Some of these new young sea-dogs of Argyll, still with the blue ganzies and the mahogany faces of the old school, are to be seen in the luxurious bar of one of the tourist hotels, having an early *apéritif* before setting out for the night's fishing. They cast off from the quay in their roomy vessels, make their shot in the night waters round Arran, and then on the morning run up Kilbrennan Sound can even lift the radio telephone instrument to call their wives or mothers in Tarbert and tell them to put the kettle on for breakfast.

None of this latter-day ease, however, was to be seen in the little town on the day of our arrival. Depression lay over the place, and was ill-concealed in the neglected mien of men and craft. 'It's too late in the year for boats like that to be out,' insisted a knot of fishermen round the canoes, in fierce justification of the lifetime of sea-lore which had left them full minds, if empty nets. We spent much time in talking there, for it was a time when the fishermen who were left were experiencing almost from day to day a double bitterness. It is bad enough to fish and catch nothing. It is worse to catch well, and to throw the fish away. This is what was happening to them. Often, after a far-ranging search in that stormy summer, they had triumphed and filled the hold, to return and find that no one would buy the catch. Here was a case and a cause for us, in what was later to become a familiar tale until a less erratic marketing technique was created. We took from their lips the restrained gall of their existence, and made it ready for print.

There followed a prodigious writing session, when we transformed a respectable little teashop into a press-room, by clearing two tables and writing industriously for the whole afternoon. Regular customers came and went, while we toiled on shamelessly, on the strength of having purchased some inexpensive food about midday. The result was three articles with which we made a tousled expedition to the post office. In the meantime the beached canoes acted as a bait for the unattached population, which gathered round them in growing numbers, tapping the canvas sides, testing their weights, and above all eager to see them water-borne. A press photographer who was holidaying in Tarbert spent a day-long vigil among the onlookers, sending relays of messengers in search of us to urge us afloat. His presence gave a superior cachet to the occasion, and we hastened to gratify the rising demands of the public by launching away, and posing in various paddling attitudes. Eventually, wedged afresh with loaves of bread, pots of jam, and a splaying hand of sausages, we got truly aboard.

The shaking of warning heads among the done fishermen was less obvious than the little cheer that wafted us away from the heart of the town, with the high church belfry striking a dissonant five o'clock. We had a youthful shore *cortège* of cyclists along the pier road close to our passage, until we crossed the sudden narrowing harbour bar and slanted over to the houseless north shore. There we rounded the limpet-pocked heads of the bay and came into the full flood of the tide up Loch Fyne, and a grey and sliding swell.

Our course was a ten-mile paddle due north to Loch Gilp and Ardrishaig, where the Crinan Canal begins. The Canal opens the door to the Atlantic for smaller shipping travelling from the Clyde. Our halting-place for the night was to be with my kinsfolk the MacTavishes at Castleton, and as the wooded hill of Shirvan grew towards our bows all that evening, I could yield myself readily to an intimate apprehension of our calmly planned purpose in the voyage—to reveal and explore, not a foreign uncharted land, but the alien familiarity of our own places. The night was golden, heavy with the sun. There was no help from the wind, which puffed coldly off the east. Our activities in Tarbert had been too public to permit us to cut and prepare sandwiches in the eye of the populace—although we were later to intrude our domesticities in a less bashful fashion. So we chilled a little as we stopped two miles off the shore and sliced heartily into a loaf. Loch Fyne was smooth and empty, but for us. Not even a rowing-boat out for the twilight rise of the cuddies—the saithe—competed with us for the lordship of the water. It looked a dead and a done sea indeed. And yet, because created things always do blunderingly what they have done before, in a year or two the place was to swarm with fish and fishermen. And in a year or two later it was to roar with the craft and weapons of an army, whetting John Splendid's sword for the old business of the foreign wars.

It was deep twilight when we crept round the islands of Castleton Bay and grounded below the house. Then we were in the big kitchen with its great fire and the inside timber staircase leading overhead to the loft bedroom. Here presided my Great-aunt Mary, Duncan's mother, over eighty and blind, and the question she put to me about our journey had the simple perspective of age: 'Could you get nothing better to do?' It was not, to be sure, a question which demanded an answer, for she had a long lifetime of experience in the caprices of those of her household and its offshoots. They had all, in their time, come home to her roof; and here was I, at the beginning of an exploration into the hidden aspects of a familiar land, sitting at the fireside that warmed half my roots, and more.

And Duncan. At this time he was the Joint County Clerk

of Argyll, a lean, tall, dark Celt who was an epic in himself. He did not live to hear an official of the county tell me: 'It was Duncan MacTavish who brought Argyll through the war.' The odd claim would have amused him, although he killed himself proving it. As a youth he had come from the croft and been a rare scholar at Glasgow University, winning a famous scholarship to Oxford. But he refused it, for he did not want to go to Oxford. He wanted to stay in Scotland, and he became the village master at a tiny school in the north of the county of Argyll. With the Kaiser's war he endured, for conscience' sake, a gross range of humiliations, including forced navvy labour on the road outside his school. When peace came they let him go, a silent youth, and he went back to the croft.

Soon there was a meagre clerkship in the county office, in Lochgilphead, and he worked there. His splendid mind was irresistible, and that was how, at the start of the Hitler war, he was able to gather up into his brown hands a great part of the adminstration of his beloved and scattered Argyll. Before I knew him, he was a legend of my childhood, with his Gaelic songs and poems. Later I was to learn of his real scholarship, and how the books he published, and the researches he made, were but fragments in preparation for a great history of Argyll he would have written. In the end it was to be his portion rather to make and to take part in the history of Argyll, than to write it. On long-spaced occasions I shared the inwardness of his mind, and his laughter, as we fished the saithe of the Liath Eilean rocks, or scythed his meadow hay. And yet, by the time I had at last grown towards him, and knew his ardent height, he had gone on ahead into the quiet change.

Seumas and I slept that night in sheets in a familiar bedroom looking to the bay, and were not up before the middle of the morning. Duncan had cycled off early to his Saturday forenoon's work in the county offices. He was back before lunch to take us out to the Big Island across the dried-out bay, and down to the ledges on the south tip where the seals were basking. In the early afternoon came more of our MacTavishes from the houses round about to help us in the carrying of the laden canoes across the tidal sand to the water. We took our farewells and got our blessings, especially from Great-aunt Mary, who gave us a gay and heartening send-off. I was never to see her again, and I think that, with the foreseeing gift which she and many of her people possess, she knew it.

It was a sparkling three-mile run over to Ardrishaig. At this township on an arm of Loch Fyne is the start of the Crinan Canal, and the passage of this link would deliver us into the heart of the Western Islands. We travelled in the company of a cool sun, which makes all travel endurable. Arran and Ardlamont Point were again to the south, with the excellence of picture postcards. There were glittering lumps of waves, mere superficial sports of water with no weight behind them, and we took time to photograph each other, the blue-painted canoes merging into the sea's colour, and behind them the heights of Knapdale. During most of the journey we were also engaged in a planning conference relating to our progress on the far side of the canal. The canal itself we faced with an almost apologetic sense of anticipation, hoping that any public we might have by this time would excuse our passage through these tame waters, and set-off their soft seclusion against the strenuous routes which lay ahead. This attitude, as we were to discover, was a serious underestimate of the effort necessary to negotiate the Crinan Canal, and we would shortly know more of this.

The canal starts at a sea-lock in Ardrishaig harbour, and runs almost due north for about two miles parallel to the main road, along the shallowing shore of Loch Gilp. One of our early confident theories had been that the passage of canals would not only be extremely simple to us, but would demonstrate in a conclusive way the special merit of our canoes. This was another claim which had been prominently featured in that celebrated first article written by Seumas: 'Our canoes are portable,' he had declared. 'We carry them round the locks!' Since the penning of these brave words, a warning note had been struck by our arm-wrenching experience at Bowling on the day of departure. But, we felt, we had travelled far, and hardened, since then. We were now salt-water men, and it would take more than canals to affright us. We cunningly steered a course as far into Loch Gilp as the tide would allow, and grounded eventually at a spot half a mile north of the pier, thereby skipping the first group of locks, and leaving only a stretch of shore, sand, and canal bank over which the canoes would have to be carried before they could be launched in the canal.

4. THE CRINAN CANAL SEA-LOCKS

The Dorus Mor is the gap on the near horizon above and a little to the left of the fishing boat in the loch. Craignish is on the right, and far behind it the hills of Mull. On the left above the hotel a dip in the skyline marks the Gulf of Corrievreckan.

5. THE ATLANTIC BRIDGE AT CLACHAN.

The tide was at its lowest, and the stretch of jagged foreshore which lay between us and the road was long indeed. A group of young men hastened off the highway and gathered above the tidemark to watch us arrive. We splashed ashore, each man getting his canoe as far out of the water as he could manage single-handed. Then we bent to our toil.

We had found by this time that the best method of lifting a loaded canoe by a two-man snatch was for us to stand, one on each side of the cockpit, bend and reach well below the hull, and with fingers hooked over one of the keel strips, lift, walking crabwise in the direction of the pointing bow. On a slimy foreshore at low tide, in light canvas shoes pulled on over bare feet, and on a footing which—as on most west-coast shores—was sharp and sizable boulders rather than pebbles, this was a galling labour. Each of us, lurching for a foothold, found it impossible to avoid nudging the other in mid-step, so that a safely braced stride was achieved only by a rigid push or pull which staggered the fellow-bearer. Toes were bent excruciatingly into sharp clefts; ankles and shins were ravaged; and we passed the higher boulders, not by stepping up on them, which would have tilted the whole four-legged beast to destruction, but by kneeling on them, offering the shrinking flesh to the convex caress of limpets and barnacles. There is also, in the whole posture of two people straining together above a narrow beam, a facial proximity which tries the humour. In this way we wagged up the shore with the canoes in relays. At the limit of endurance we would lower one burden on to the beach, and go back for the other, hoping to carry it farther. Between each relay we paused to recover, for lengthening intervals.

To the lads on the beach our distress was obvious, and at first only their shyness and our pride prevented a rally of helpers. Eventually their diffidence broke down only a moment before ours. 'Come on and give them a hand!' said one, and they plunged in a courteous flock towards us, sensibly shod, and heaved the canoes up the beach and over the road like battering rams going for a city wall. We were left behind, weak and shaking in the knees, shouldering our paddles like pikemen discarded in a foray.

We saw the canoes parked on the sloping canal-bank, surrounded by a growing crowd of which our helpers formed a proprietary nucleus. Seumas and I went to the canal office to bargain for the use of the water, bringing a still persuasive enthusiasm to our assurances that none of the lock gates would require to be opened for our passage. 'We carry them round the locks!' Mr. Livingstone, the very able executive who ushers the varied traffic of the canal on its way, had read the words himself in the *Daily Record* a week ago. He charged nothing, and sped us on our way in an encouraging manner, as he does to such a range of craft.

Shortly, we were dipping the canoes afloat, and were off paddling up the canal. We were glad to be moving, for a cold wind was coming from the north-west, strongly enough to push at our faces and to set us swinging strenuously at the paddles. There seems always to be a wind, and a headwind at that, in our Scots canals, channelled as they are in the isthmus clefts which nature has not quite finished off. It is always a cold wind, and, lacking the rhythm and the courtesy of the sea-winds, plucks frontally at a canoeist and tries to break his heart.

A canoeist on a canal is a very low form of nautical life, overlooked by even small children on the banks, while the waterway, edging past the ends of villa gardens, rarely loses a suburban character. It is no place to enjoy the spacious privacy which is at least one of exploration's assets. We hastened on, hoping to be quickly done with this useful but ridiculous journey. Ladies lifted aside the curtains of their back windows to watch us battle past, fighting headwinds and red in the face. Strollers on the towing path paced up more briskly to talk to us, and we had pains to let them fall behind. These self-inflicted combats with pedestrians brought on a sense of exasperation which the wind fanned to a disproportionate fury.

Soon Oakfield Bridge appeared ahead, and with it a piquant navigational problem. The bridge has no more than a foot or two of clearance above the water, and as we had left our masts stepped, their trifling height was sufficient to prevent a passage under. Numbers of passers-by accumulated to watch us surmount the obstacle, and their speculations were as vague as our own. We attempted first of all to lever ourselves under by grasping the girders and heaving the canoes over on their sides so that the masts lay almost parallel with the water, and so out of the way of the overhead obstruction. We were all disappointed when this failed, baffled by the sheer buoyancy of the canoes. With sweating nonchalance Seumas and I came alongside in mid-canal to unship each other's mast, a ruse which would have been acclaimed, had it succeeded. But the unseasoned timber of the broom handles had now stuck them in their sockets, and we revolved slowly in the water, baffled and tiring, and twisting in vain at the mast-poles with desperate fists.

A later reflection bade us paddle to the bank, land, and partially unpack the canoes, as the only sure method of freeing the masts. As we landed, a young girl came forward, presented each of us with a bunch of white heather, and asked for our autographs. It was a kindly act; and especially at that moment. It gave us, even in our impotence, some sort of standing on the remote fringes of celebrity. We tied the heather to our bows with gestures as courtly as we could perform; signed with a cramped flourish; ripped the masts from their bedfast lairs; bundled aboard, and, paddling like steamboats, surged under the low girders of the bridge and onwards inland.

Here we turned to the westward among the hills, leaving Loch Fyne behind. The towing path was now left to cyclists, going down to the cinema in Lochgilphead. As the light dwindled we came up towards Cairnbaan, and the long ladder of locks on which the canal climbs to its summit. Below the first lock we came ashore, flipping the canoes half on to the bank while we prospected the hurdles ahead. A rapid cunning was now informing our minds on the transport of canoes. Already the 'carry them round the locks' theory was without credit. Any canal banks we have met are steep and slippery pitches, affording to the bearers of a loaded canoe every refinement of a prodigious labour as they manhandle it up and down. As for the spaces between the locks of a series, they are just too short to justify the scramble up and down to make paddling use of the intervening stretches of water. A group of five locks, as at Cairnbaan, will cover about five hundred yards. To pass it without sailing through the locks, one of two labours must be undertaken. The first is to emerge at the first lock, portage along the whole towing path, and re-enter the water beyond the last lock. The second is to paddle over all the intervening water, leaving a total portage of perhaps 200 yards—enough to go round the lock gates only—

as well as five cliff-like launchings and landings. These are hard alternatives indeed.

We had, however, as we thought, learned our lesson. So we strolled up to the top of the ladder of locks, and there chose a site for the tent, in view of the canal and of some of the picturesque houses which are here ribbon-built along the water. A brief foray among the houses yielded a borrowed wheelbarrow, and this we trundled with some smugness back to the canoes, wearing the aspect of men whom experience has taught, but not embittered. Shortly we were awheel with the first canoe up the considerable incline towards Cairnbaan village and our camp site.

We did our transportation here on the main road, rather than on the towing path. The canoe lay beamwise on the barrow, which had to take the crown of the road while its 14-foot cargo spread its horns abroad, blocking the passage of the road to all other transport. Nevertheless, this was a luxurious form of portage, and we were at once devotees of the barrow. At times a car would sweep on us with the verve of Highland transport, forcing us to a quick turn of ninety degrees and a panic trundle towards the ditch, into which our barrow's wheel bit to the axles. But the labour of hauling it up again to the summit of the considerable camber was trifling to what would have been involved in launching and landing. We made the journey twice, and got the tent up. It was an evening of lovely calm, but murderous with midges. The tent door had to be closed, denying ourselves the view, while turf and fragments of peat, reeking on the top of a stove, set up a choking diversion. With the return of the wind in the night the menace blew away.

In a fresh and splendid Sunday morning we got away again, hoping to make Crinan and an early afternoon flood-tide on the same day. Crinan Canal is a sweet waterway, carved here over a narrow neck of country which once, before the land tilted, was probably a tidal sea-way. It runs round the bases of heather rocks and through lochans which feed the channel from the hill burns. There was no lingering possible for us in the darling nooks which cried for lazing among the willows and the reeds, and we flogged on to Dunardary and the next ladder of locks. These stepped now downwards to the sea-level, and from the top the sea itself was visible, out towards the Sound of Jura. A south-easterly wind was gentle but steady. We would be there for that tide and that wind.

At Dunardary we went confidently to find a barrow, and failed. There was not a barrow in the place, or at least, not one which would come out on Sunday. The keeper of one of the top locks was helpful in remembering a handcart which lay in a near-by quarry, and we went with him to inspect it. It was not difficult to find, with its solid iron wheels bedded deeply in the mud and grasses. A great tree with a crosspiece formed the traction system, ready for the grasp of mighty hands and thews. It had no sides, and the massive planking which formed the flat platform of the cargo space was thickly coated with ancient dried cement. It was like a vehicle which might have been used to haul stones to the Great Pyramid. We had been wiser to leave it; but the triumph of wheeled transport remained with us from the night before, and we laid inadequate hands on the find. With the lock-keeper and some boys helping and heaving, we worked the thing loose from its setting and got it, creaking hideously, on to the towpath. With one of the canoes poised and rolling slightly on the flat top, the *cortège* heaved down the incline to the end of the locks. It was long since our tumbril had moved, and to push it downhill took as much effort as should have been necessary to push it uphill. We pressed onwards heavily, too proud now to admit failure, while watchers from the cottages regarded the penance, some of them no doubt with satisfaction, thinking of the day it was. · The unloading of the canoe at the other end caused no discernible lightening of the load, and the return journey was ghastly to contemplate. We bent to it at last: and when, after an infinite effort, we reached again the quarry entrance, we sent our vehicle lurching down towards its former bed. It is questionless still there. We carried the second canoe down.

From there we had a lock-free run to Crinan, fringing the great moss where kings used to hunt below the walls of Dunadd, and where now the herds of cattle feed and grow fat. We were the only traffic, since the canal closes on Sunday. Nowadays the Crinan waterway is known only to yachts and puffers on their various business up and down the West Coast. At one time, when canals were popular and cars had not begun, there was a 'roomy, elegant, and well-appointed steamboat' linking with steamer services at both ends of the canal. These were once busy tourist waters, and may well be so again. Even the *Comet*, the first steamboat that ever went to sea, made passenger runs here, and was wrecked in the tide race of the Dorus Mor.

We swept in independent triumph below the bridge at Islandadd, where canal boats have baffling experiences as they await the opening; on through the strange surprise of Bellanoch Bay; and then, on a shelf of water, round the base of Crinan hill and on to the last locks before the sea. Here we lifted the canoes out and carried them down to a landing-stage, to leave them lying among the seaweed. Saving time, we ate lunch in the hotel, among the Sabbath crowds of car parties from Glasgow and other urban centres, ourselves bare-legged, and slippered in canvas shoes from which our toes were peeping, to anticipate a fashion since popular in superior hotels.

From the dining-room window could be seen the whole start of the road to the west where we were to go: Loch Crinan and its near islets; Loch Craignish, a charming diversion into the heart of the land; the rougher road seaward through the Dorus Mor, where we would turn sharp to the north; ahead still, and farther, was the gap of Corryvreckan, pillared by Scarba and Jura; still and away beyond was the promise of Mull; and in our scraps and slats of canvas and wood we would leave all these far behind. So at least ran the programme; and so, in the event, it was to be. But on such a day, with the sea and the wind going too, it looked easier than we deserved.

CHAPTER VI

THE DORUS MOR

> This was our time that we took—
> We, on that day, and no others;
> The wind was a friend for the look
> He laid on the sail as it shook,
> And the sea said—'Come then, brothers!'

THE Dorus Mor (the Great Door) was likely to be our biggest immediate difficulty. We knew of it already. Campbell the Pilot had told us to pass it at slack water, but some local guidance seemed desirable. It is a half-mile gap of water between the mainland Point of Craignish and the island of Garbh Reisa. Here the tide, running irregularly round the island and meeting in the gap on the other side—meeting at different speeds because of the parting it has suffered—tumbles among itself at the reunion and creates a miniature Corrievreckan. We were doubtful whether our craft could negotiate the place, and whether a flood-tide would be the best condition for the attempt.

This was the problem we put to a crew of Clyde herring fishermen whom we found by good fortune in the canal basin (going south, the wise men!) and they waved the caution aside with broad and reassuring gestures. 'Take it at the flood!' they said it heartily, more than once, 'and one tide'll carry you right to Oban.' This nautical wisdom was confident, and also welcome, and we gladly laid aside our misgivings. It was now about three in the afternoon, and a bonny blue-skied day, with the tide turning in slack water, ready to flood.

The wind was southerly, looking as if it might remain steadily at our backs for the first time. So we stepped the masts again and rigged sail, looking forward to an effortless passage and a triumphant evening arrival in Oban, about thirty miles away. There was a launching scramble first among the low weedy rocks which the deep tide had left, and then we were away, paddling with the bows on the Dorus Mor, opening for us clear and inviting seven miles ahead.

Within half a mile out from the shore we could feel the insistent help of the wind almost behind us. It was a glorious moment as we shipped paddles, heaved up the sails by their paltry strings, and felt the sudden benevolent twitch as we went on steadily under sail. This was an interval for luxury, and we reclined at incredible ease in our cockpits, never dipping a paddle for the next mile or two, except for a momentary steering correction, while the canoes slid ahead with us at a good paddling pace. There was warmth at last in the sun, and it seemed truly as if our first stages might well prove to have been the worst.

Crinan was dwindling astern; the little bays of Kilmartin shore opened and closed on our right as we passed them; Craignish opened to the north, but its soft harbourage was not for us, and we knew it without regret. We scraped the little Island of Dogs, and felt ourselves to be on the actual threshold of the open sea. After the first well and surge of this sentiment we set to paddling, and pushed ourselves forward at what seemed to be the most perfect of all speeds, which is fast enough. The waves were growing now behind us, lifting us and running along beneath to escape from under the bows and leave us in a trough, which also travelled with us part of the way, until a new wave was elected to rise astern. We took to racing these wave children, going with them in little bursts, and laughing as they did. For this was innocent water. In the full opening of Loch Craignish we appeared to be hastening even more. Bigger waves now lifted and carried us briefly, and although we did not guess the force of it then, the tide was urging us onward faster.

The doorway of the Dorus Mor was widening and nearing, with a black line like a step across the entrance. This line appeared at first to be merely our normal horizon, which was unusually limited because of the low level of the canoes. But as we approached, it did not appear to recede. Indeed, it thickened and rose markedly above the normal height of the horizon water all round—a phenomenon making for sudden unease. Our approach was swifter now, and, straining towards the forbidding dark barrier at the gap, our closer vision decomposed it into a sudden moving turbulence, as if mighty fish were distantly shoaling in the Dorus. From a mile off we could

THE DORUS MOR 49

see the separate spouts and breakers which, in extreme miniature, would have been a sign of mackerel. And as we peered and pondered, borne along, a lull in the wind sucked back to us the noise of a sea tumult.

We hauled down the sails and bundled them at the foot of the masts, slowing our speed. But by this time we were fairly in the race, and the noisy thresh of it filled all our hearing for the minutes that were to intervene before it cast us out beyond Craignish Point. The water changed in colour from a pleasant green to a sudden and sullen black, in which writhed streamers and trails of spent foam. And with the colour went the one-way rhythm of the water which had taken us here. The lifting waves that had followed and passed us in reliable attendance were drowned in a jauping popple. These separate wave-peaks reared individually and fell on us, punching at our sides and canvas tops, each one jerking us as solidly as a thrown bucket of stones.

'Keep paddling!' we shouted, although we had probably better have shipped paddles and given ourselves to the flood. Yet at that moment we had not realised that we were still travelling at the full speed of the tide. Dipping paddles, and tugging and staring at the near water, we appeared to be fixed and struggling in a static maelstrom. A glance farther ahead corrected the impression, for onwards, and approaching, was a low wall of water, higher than the level we were on, where the two irregular tide forces were heaving up the sea between them.

The wall seemed to dart and strike us, although it was we who rushed on it. Here the paddles felt new forces that made them kick in our grip as if hands in the water had seized to wrestle them from us. We were now in a moving group of whirlpools, and the noise was a hissing thunder. On the other side of our hulls of cloth and slats the sea gathered below our thighs like a horse bunching for the gallop. I struck the perimeter of a great swirl, swooped half round it and rammed Seumas with my point on his bow, remorselessly, although we were both stroking fiercely apart. We clashed together for a moment along the length of the hulls, and parted on our ways again. Several times there would come a sudden subsidence of the near water, leaving one or other of the canoes sliding on the surface of a smooth bubble platform of sea, twenty yards across, pressed inches higher than the surrounding level like a lily-leaf adrift. Then this would burst and rip across and the spouts would storm at us, and a force below would seem to twitch the canoes deeply down below what buoyancy still ruled them.

By this time we had ceased to fight with our paddles, using them more as balance against the rocking, which was too extreme to control. So, looking up, we had time to notice our onward progress, and to wonder why we still floated. As if to emphasise the movement, I was plucked round in a swirl like a giant circus roundabout, and found myself sweeping past the little cliffs of Craignish Point. They were only a few feet away, and they seemed to go past my face like the wall of a railway tunnel seen from a carriage window, the stuck limpets appearing like blurred white lines.

This was the last kick of the race, for here we burst through the narrowest neck of the channel and were disgorged into freer water, leaving the noise and threat of the Dorus Mor gradually behind us. There was still enough press in the flood to send us, spent and swirling, close up the rocks on the far side of Craignish. This entry we made to the Sound of Jura had surprise for at least one citizen of that sparse landscape. A kilted man was standing in a seaward-looking pose on the very point of the land—'Long Looking to Jura', as the Gaelic song says—when we came surging up on him from behind and were vomited out of the tide race almost at his feet. In the polite county of Argyll, it must have been shock, and no lack of grace, which made him unable to return our drenched salute. He stared and stared after us as we drifted out of his sight up the fringes of the Craignish rocks.

There is an elation which follows novel perils, and we savoured it as we sang and laughed, or called down wet curses on the fishermen who had advised us to take the Dorus Mor on the flood-tide. Later we were to come to know full and open seas, and to feel trust in their directional rhythm. But we had been into a brew, where the twisting and clapping together of the erratic water could easily have sunk us. It was on that day we lost a large part of trust in local knowledge, and were made to take our own judgments, for our own needs at least. In spite of these heavy considerations, we were very pleased with ourselves for this progress and experience. Baling and sponging out the several inches of water in which we sat, we ate sandwiches and were merry at our ease for a time, while the tide swelled steadily north and took us with it. Some miles farther to the west, choked between the ramparts of Jura and Scarba, the feared Gulf of Corrievreckan, with its whirlpool and overfalls, was settling in to its incessant tidal torments. But although we fancied we heard its renowned roaring, 'like a thousand chariots', as the old description runs, we felt none of the legendary force in the sea plucking us towards it. Our route was now due north to Seil Sound, between the mainland and the isle called Reisa Mhic Phaidean, into Shuna Sound and on to the narrows of Seil, spanned by the Atlantic Bridge. We were getting the wind now free again, a little easterly of south, and up went the sails. They grasped the wind into their full little bellies, and we set off darting on our way.

So we sailed all that afternoon until the light and the tide were done. We felt, and I think we still feel, that there will never be another sail like that. It never happened again in the many weeks more of our travels, and they will be lucky indeed who know of such joy anywhere, finding together in one occasion the wind, the tide, the boat, and the time to take them all. There was never an instant's slackening of the wind, and as the hours passed its force grew lightly but steadily. Our paddles became mere steering oars. The scraps of sail, straining into galley shape, were golden because the sun was warm on them and us. The land around was in a daze of colour, and the waves were indigo, going with us, swelling and growing in the wider sea and bigger wind, and bursting their tops, first slowly and then often, into incredible white. Soon a fair sea was running, rocking us steeply back and forward, as they overran and pushed past us.

Shortly an astounding sensation came to us—one of which we had never heard, and which we set at once to master and enjoy. The waves were now breaking heavily all round. Several times they burst just as they were overtaking us, so that the forward spout of surf would throw us bodily ahead on our course, to travel for a few seconds in and with the breaker. We yielded to these urges, and even assisted them by paddling, until a new ecstasy was suddenly born. We found that we could surf-ride on the open sea. It meant keeping a stern-wise eye for an overtaking wave which was about to break, and manœuvring and paddling so that the explosion came about half-way along the stern point. We could thus lay the canoes forward on the wave like surfboards, and by paddling and sailing stay on the curl of the breaker until it had died away. We were hardly perfect in this trick when an extension came. As the breaker subsided, a new one was born somewhere half a stroke away from its fragments, and with a leap we could get aboard this second comber. There is a fever of the spirit which brings expertness, sometimes, as a quick reward. It seemed a few minutes only when we were riding five or six breakers in succession, each one springing living from the frothy embers of the last, and pausing to let us get astride before it rolled forward. We found that six at a time was the limit, and we were never able to do more in immediate succession. After that number the impetus of one particular wave-stream had died away, and a new phase would start too far off on our beam to let us aboard. In time, however—minutes only—a new phase would work round and be surging up behind us.

The forward speed was tremendous in sensation. We weltered along, up to the elbows in the bursting surf. As the waves grew steeper and stronger, the forward-pointing slant of the canoe drove the whole bow point under, and the craft would tear the sea apart like the coulter of a plough. One had the impression of watching from its own periscope a diving submarine. The stern points lifted clean out, and the strain on our slender bracing wires must have been enormous. As the wind rose constantly, ripping us through Shuna Sound, our dolphin darts among the rising surf bore us forward on the breakers at the very speed of the waves. Seumas, catching his own series of waves, would soar ahead of me as I merely sailed, his stern point cocked up at the peak force of the wave burst; then his paddles would revolve for a violent moment as he poised to take the next; up he would heave again, and away on the black-and-white roller; and so, jerked forward by wave after wave, when the series died he would be a hundred and fifty yards ahead of me. And as he was left, my own clan of waves would sally up astern and rush me towards and past him. As the weight of the breeze stiffened, we reefed up the sails until they were smaller than sheets of newspaper. They still pulled us on, bending over to the streams of bubbles foaming from the sunk bow, or raising their tight arcs to the sky as each smooth wave, its breaker exhausted, lifted the bow to prance free from our straddling as we rode it.

THE DORUS MOR

In this way we were soon into the narrow channel of Shuna Sound, between the island of that name and the larger island of Luing, and the weather still ran us directly northwards. Shuna, on our right, was getting the sun on all its flanks that faced us, and seemed to gather into its park-like variety all the immense ranges of colour which make such a day unforgettable. On our left, Luing, one of the Slate Islands, ran a long tongue of land up to its mate Seil. We came in closer to Luing shore to get a new sight of Toberonochy village, and as we came in view of the houses we were seen and signalled round all the community, glad no doubt to have a Sunday afternoon diversion. People gathered thickly upon the pier, and a great waving and shouting set up, to which we replied with upheld paddles.

'Come in here!' came a clear call, cutting the wind, and a chime of shouted welcomes followed. It was a tempting moment. But we were (rightly, as it turned out) too greedy of the fortunate wind, and determined to make it carry us to its last gasp. We bucked on past the bay, with parting flourishes of the paddles, and the fringe of white houses crept back into the mass of land. On the whole trip we never left a spot unvisited with more reluctance.

Clearing the north point of Shuna, we felt the wind backing more firmly to the east, tending to push us westwards and giving us the steering troubles to be expected in a keelless boat with a wind hinting to the beam. It went round only gradually, however, and there were still a few miles of robust sailing to come. We were scantily clad, and the edged wind was chilling our soaked backs. So we paddled most of the time, and moved even faster than before. At Degnish Point we could see right into the heart of Loch Melfort, opening inland, and then we had the mainland close on our right hand and were again in a small channel. A mile or two farther, and Cuan Sound, the favourite yacht passage between Luing and Seil, opened narrowly on our left, leading out to the Firth of Lorne. Only very small craft could continue on the route to which we now held, still north, with Seil Sound closing in on us on both sides.

Freaks of wind spilled over the lumps of hill which lined our way, and pressed us shorewards on the Seil side. The canoes would heel suddenly to port, and we would have to strike hard with the right-hand paddle to bring them round and let them run more before the wind until the end of the gust. With this, and our erratic riding of the surf as it came, we got widely separated, and I was far ahead when Balvicar Bay opened to the left, with the houses on the south shore, and the road visible as it ran to the Atlantic Bridge and Oban beyond. At the far end of the bay Seil Sound suddenly narrowed to a river width, and the sun was gone. Here a roaring gust hit me and would have had me over into my running wake had I not slipped the cord holding up the sail. The little rag blew straight out like a banner, and I lost way and got my balance. There was big force in the wind now, and I pulled in the sail and bundled it, cold, but gloating at the ceaseless run from Craignish. I turned to wait for Seumas, and he wasn't there. There was no canoe on the mile or so of water I could see clearly astern. In the hope that he would be sheltering somewhere, to take down his sail also, I waited in the small congested rollers, dipping paddles enough to keep me from losing ground to the tide. After ten minutes there was still no sign of him, and I started back, with the chill and the fear of disaster making great play on my nerves, already taut with the tension of the passage.

I heaved a desperate course back for a wet half-mile, and it took long, with the wind and the tide ahead. There is nothing in the world emptier than water from which a boat has vanished. In despair, and tired, I heard Seumas hail from a tiny entrance ahead, and he came out paddling and beaming characteristically. He had been struck by the gust which had heeled me, but had plucked in vain at his sail sheet. The elementary slip-knots we employed could not deal with saltwater-soaked blind cord, and with the sail jammed aloft, and pulling its fill of gale wind, he had had to turn away before it. The gust drove him planing up a lucky creek, and ashore—not, fortunately, on the rocks, but bedded fast in a swamp of rushes. He could neither paddle nor sail out of this refuge, and had spent some time plucking himself forth, rending loose a whole harvest of rushes in the coming. He talked with gusto of the final burst of speed he had achieved before the landing, with the canoe standing on its side-boards and leaving even the speediest wave behind.

Now it was a deep dusk, and the wind was painful to hear in the narrows. We left the sails down, paddling along easily, borne by the tide, and even sailing before the wind force catching at our backs. The Seil houses grew more frequent on our left as we passed the separate hamlets, and lads ran for their bicycles and pedalled along the shore road on our level, hailing ahead of us like an advance guard. In this way we accumulated a following, and when, in a mile or two, we saw in great eagerness the high arch of the bridge, it was battlemented with the heads and shoulders of the people.

The last of the flood-tide swept us up to the bridge, and as we turned in to land by the hotel, almost the only building here, men ran down the grass towards us. As a last rocket of wind shot us abreast and bumping on the shore, one put a large hand on each bow and pulled both canoes clear, saying levelly: 'Well, you're here!'

Shortly, while the hotel cooked a meal we would remember, we bathed. Longer than the meal, I shall have a recollection of Seumas, sitting in the bath with scalding water to his neck, and his emergent head (indeed, all of him) as red as a lobster. He simply sat there, and wallowed, and grinned with salty bleariness through the steam; and would not come out of it, until the cook, pounding on the bathroom door and crying kitchen havoc, almost broke in.

And all night, whenever we stirred, it was to hear the air full of the noise of the gale. Close by our bedroom window in the hotel ran a cluster of telephone wires, from which, incessantly, came a vicious and malevolent harping.

CHAPTER VII

THE ISLES

> With days at their worst to hinder and harry me,
> Summerland calls, and naething shall tarry me;
> Wind from the dawning sun westwards shall carry me
> Back to the Islands of Glory.
>
> There's glory of sun and glory of thundering,
> Glory of storm that I worship in wondering;
> Glamour of cities will no more be sundering
> Me from the Islands of Glory.

SEIL is an island, but only just. It is separated from the mainland of Argyll by the Sound, which for some miles of its length is no wider than a hard-running river, betraying itself by the salt smell, and the seaweed below the tide. A century and a half ago, the high arch of the Clachan Bridge was flung across at the place which was an ebb ford, and, spanning an undoubted arm of the ocean, it gathered a tourist renown as 'the only bridge across the Atlantic Ocean'. At the time of our visit the plans were well ahead for the bridging of the Hebridean South Ford between Benbecula and South Uist, and with the building of that second span there are at least two places where the picturesque claim can be made, to say nothing of Achill Island in Ireland, a footbridge at Canna, and some modest projects of a similar kind in Canada. The Clachan Bridge was, however, undoubtedly the first, and intends to stick to its proud label, if the local postcards and the bus tours from Oban give any clue.

There is plenty of tidal depth and good overhead clearance at Clachan, where the builders had the local fishing craft in mind when they knit the arch together. It is a striking highway, drawing together on and across its ramparts the vivid traffic of the group of islands—squeaking and indomitable bikes; motor-cycles, oddly assembled, and driven with dash; grocers' vans, tourist buses, the mail coach, cows, cars, and lorries.

The quarries of roofing slates pit the landscapes, and all have wavered wildly in their fortunes. Easdale has the most fame and quality, and probably the most precarious history. At one time, nearly a century ago, a commune of workmen leased the quarries to work them as a co-operative enterprise, and failed to pay a dividend. Leasehold has varied to and fro, with the prospects never moving far enough back from the edge of the slump conditions which blight most endeavours in the west. A freak of wartime was the sudden appearance in Easdale of a high-grade light engineering factory.

We spent the morning in the luxury of indoors. Residence in hotels, whatever the weather, had to be a rare and diminishing treat, because of budget difficulties, and we could not afford to stay another night here, although the charges were modest enough. This morning was cruel with easterly rain and wind, which hammered even the sheltered little hotel garden. Here grew a fronded palm-tree, speaking again of the mildness of this western air, but in the high wind it was thrashing itself cruelly. Waiting for the tide, we drafted some newspaper material to be completed and sent from Oban, which we were determined to reach this time on the afternoon tide. The snug site of the hotel escaped the full blasts, and we could always hope that the day would lift with the tide.

There was no sign of this by the ebb, and we gave the returning tide half an hour to cover the bare slaty beds below the bridge. By that time the northward flow of the tide was trailing the seaweeds upstream, and it was time for us to go.

A portage, scrambling along the sharp edges of the slate packs which formed the stream-bed, allowed us to rest the canoes aground below the bridge, and we got aboard there, waiting to float off. We had misjudged the time by fifteen minutes. Prolonged slack water held back the rise, and we sat, scourged by grey rain, the least mobile boatmen which Clachan had ever seen. Happily, the only spectator of our duck-like brooding was a solitary man with a horse and cart. He stopped on the mainland side of the road to inspect, leaning his dripping cap into the rain, and peered for a time, before splashing on.

Shortly we jarred forward an inch or two, stuck again, then lifted and ran smoothly off down the channel. One or two edged snags, wigged by seaweed, but still sharp enough to pierce our hulls, held us up jolting, but the keel strips took the worst of the slashes. We were soon out of the river aspect of the sound, and into a sea bay from which the tidal rush, travelling all the way we had come yesterday, threw itself and us into the Firth of Lorne.

For a mile or two farther we had shelter from the mainland coast on our right, and the worst of the wind blew over our heads. A splendid group of islands which hold the delectable yacht anchorage of Puilldobhran grouped themselves in the drenching vista on our left. Seawards lay the biggest of them, Eileen Duin —the island of the fort—where I was able at a later time to bring in a yacht safely (after a navigator had become confused in the dusk) only because I knew the meaning of the Gaelic name and recognised its shape before night fell. On that day with the canoes, it had little shape at all, and the waves clawing its eastward side hinted at the weather which waited for us ahead. To our right the land now fell away into Loch Feochan, opening the door to a weight of wind. Ahead was a hazy four-mile stretch to the next shelter for our route, the Sound of Kerrera and the run in to Oban. It was bracing to recognise that on our left was the greatest open stretch of water we had so far sailed in, for if the day had been clear we should have seen limitlessly into the Atlantic, with the far corners of the great island of Mull as a mere milestone early on the way.

There was no occasion, however, for these satisfied reflections. Slanting right-handed into the heart of the wind, we set to the hardest two hours of our journey so far. For a spell of fully half that time we paddled only on the left hand, straining against the storm's violent pushing of our bows out to sea. We travelled in a constant outward slew, whose only corrective was this incessant heaving inwards with the left paddle, and the right blades were never dipped. So we went across the mouth of Loch Feochan like exhausted crabs, the dead weight of the wind requiring that our effort was not so much paddling as a single-arm leverage, lifting the solid canoe like an awkward bundle rather than a boat to be sweetly propelled.

Nor did we at that moment realise how solid the canoes indeed were. We had no time to make the usual halts to bale out water which poured down our flanks and accumulated below, washing some inches deep about our thighs as we sat. Such baling was, in fact, becoming an unnecessary fad. From about

THE ISLES

this time onwards, water, unless in dangerous quantities, was baled only on account of cold, and not of wetness. And on this occasion we were by no means cold.

Rain, sea-water, and sweat on the face make an uncanny blend which withdraw one gradually from the ordinary world. Not that the world is ordinary in the Firth of Lorne, and this day, as water curtains dropped and lifted patchily on all the scenery, it had the look of no known world. But there was relief coming in the tattered geography of the coast when the far point of Loch Feochan pushed at last between us and the worst of the gale.

From there we hung to the island all the way up Kerrera Sound, getting only the steady rain, and the wind in little spasms. We missed a clear sight of velvet Kerrera, with its fine little pasture valleys and shelters. It closes the bay of Oban, and is itself rich in famous harbours. In one of these assembled the Scots fleet of Alexander II when his expedition was fitting out against the Hebrides. Almost exactly seven hundred years later, in the same place, a fleet of Coastal Command Short-Sunderlands would be assembling and operating over half the Atlantic, with the Sound of Kerrera as its war base. All the sea-kings and admirals who have had business in the western waters have known the four-mile length of Kerrera. They have their remains, too. The proud shell of Gylen Castle, built by the MacDougalls a century before Alexander, commands the Firth of Lorne south-wards. Names in Gaelic and Norse remember this king and that.

Coming in towards Oban, we noted the end-of-season yachts moving uneasily at the Brandystone anchorage, and recalled that September would begin in five days. The main streets of Oban, now appearing, had an aspect which confirmed the date. Coming as we did in small boats from a desert of waters, Oban seemed to us a mighty and dripping city. We landed in the centre of it, at the stone boat-slip beside the station pier, drawing at once a cluster, and then a concourse, of bored citizens and holiday-makers glad of the diversion.

In our behaviour on arrival we fell away badly from the classic pattern outlined in the travel books. We ought to have jumped briskly ashore, run a cool eye over the natives, picked a few of the stronger ones to carry the canoes, and then shouldered a way through the jostling crowds towards the most expensive hotel.

An inability to finance such a sequence was only one of the reasons which forced a less impressive course. Not one of the spectators, to whom we granted on request several damp autographs, could have failed to outbid our total financial assets.

We stood for a moment, rain and salt water draining from the singlets and shorts which were our sole garments, and recollected that it would not be possible to pitch a tent on the esplanade of a thriving Highland town. Our first need was to change quickly, and, snatching our clothing bundles from the canoes, we strode towards the railway station, and the only free place of privacy we could think of. We were followed by the crowd, and although age and sex forced many of them to fall back at the entrance where a sign debarred all but 'Gentlemen', the younger males entered with us. In this oozy grotto we dried and were changing when the stationmaster came to rescue us with an invitation to use his own office. Here, before a fire, which we needed, we finished our dressing, and reconnoitred the town, already so well known to us.

The first concern was to find housing for the canoes, and this we arranged in a boat-shed near the Northern Lights quay. We tried to persuade the owner to allow us to sleep there with the canoes, but this was too much, in a town devoted so fully to hotels and tourist houses. Paddling the boats round the bay we left them in this place, luckier than ourselves, with a roof over their heads, while we went uphill to the landward part of the town to look for a camping site. But we pitched no tent after all. We met casually in the street a friend of Seumas who owned a boarding-house, and he played host to us for two warm-hearted days. We were able here to get a good deal of writing done in comfort, and make all ready for the next move.

A morning was spent in making much of the canoes. The period started with a bitter discovery. We had been disappointed to find that our seeming fitness and dexterity was not producing an improving travel performance. The canoes felt even more sluggish at this stage than they had done in our infinitely clumsier hands at the outset many days before. During the previous day's paddle from Clachan to Oban there had been times when they were so low in the broken water that it seemed we had to incorporate a downward thrust in our paddling to force the bows out of the water and enable them to meet and lift to onward waves. As they lay in the boat-house at Oban, empty of our equipment, it was a strain for the two of us to lift even one of them. We unstranded the canoes at last and separated each into its three sections. The four end-points fell heavily to the ground—the buoyancy tanks, the sealed life-savers! —and would hardly be lifted. Each one was swilling half full of sea-water, which jostled from end to end inside like a knell as the section was rocked. There had been a steady seepage where the composition fabric joined the timber bulwarks, and from each separate bow and stern point we poured the fill of two buckets of water. We did this with a great sense of elation also, as the traveller must when some heavy defect in his equipment is detected and simply remedied. So we learned a very simple principle of ship construction—perfection is keeping the water out; efficiency is keeping it from staying in. We bought several collapsible tubes of cement and fixed down our canvas again. Thereafter, every day or two, we took the canoe sections apart, prised a suitable bilge-hole where the fabric met the wooden framework, and emptied out the sample we carried of the waters safely passed. The flap was then gummed down again.

In any part of the Highlands, even in a well-poised little metropolis like Oban, such a running repair was bound to create interest, and also scepticism. This was especially marked in the case of Mr. Duncan MacDougall, who sold us the tubes of cement. As a thriving ship's chandler, ironmonger, and general merchant, he was accustomed to a more orthodox process of boat maintenance. In such districts merchandising is something more than shopkeeping. A store is near to the old style of trading post, and there was always, it seemed to me, a special adventure in the Oban shops. One of them had a slogan long before these sales devices were common, and it had often braced my boyhood newspaper reading—'everything from a trout fly to a steam yacht'. The claim seemed so much more dashing than 'from a needle to an anchor' that I had long looked forward to doing business in such an emporium. Here was my ambition fulfilled. We were personally attended by the proprietor, and for the most part treated almost as seamen, although our order (for patent gum to stick our boats together) was trifling, if not humiliating. He had been to have a look at the canoes, and quizzed us on our plans and route, saying levelly: 'You'll not go far. This is the last we'll see of you!' And again, pointing to the pillars of cold rain that moved and fell across the bay: 'The weather's broken for good. There'll be no more summer now for your nonsense. It's too late in the year!' But this was said more as a gesture to the general opinion, and not from any original gloom. He had a good twinkle of benevolence for us in all our meetings, and on our way south in November, when the voyage was over, he greeted us with great heartiness and a play of mock-relief.

We got away some fat packets by post to the newspapers. The whole of the West was thoroughly alert to our coming, as all our news messages, telling our progress from place to place, were being well recorded. Such adventure as we had found it expedient to describe had lost nothing in the sub-editing. The porpoises in Loch Fyne, and the perils of the Dorus Mor, were strenuously featured, and our unbowed heads were reproduced from the departure pictures in a style which could assist neither identity nor sympathy. At Oban, we found time to write some more purposive articles, holding a note of authority on our main theme—the condition of the West and its people.

Apart from this writing, and the shock repairs to the canoes, there was nothing to keep us here. In the summer Oban has the air always of a well-doing coastal resort, and certainly, at that time, the casual visitor could hardly have guessed at a hinterland of marginal farming and crofting threatened constantly by poverty and bedevilled by the booms and slumps which punched our food producers into a constant depression. Oban takes some pride in its west-endy label 'The Charing Cross of the Highlands', and has equipped itself for a career of tourism. There are splendid hotels—tashed a little in the war—and the taste and display of certain of the shops show forth a dignity capable of earning handsome rewards, if Scotland were to make a major industry of tourism. In such a setting, and encouraged by the eager demands of its visitors, Oban has developed some sense of pageantry, and might well allow this spirit to have its fling. The Oban Games, held in an arena whose grandstands are a ring of cliffs, are probably the best-staged event of the kind outside of Deeside. Oban is the sort of place which might well produce a voice to speak resoundingly for the West. There has been no sign of such an emergence. In a social sense, Oban's best contribution to the adjacent Highlands is the virile sponsorship of its shinty teams. And, shinty being a winter game, the tourist rarely sees its effect.

The canoes were noticeably lighter, and biddable to our paddling, as we thrust them out of Oban Bay on the last Wednesday of August. For the past two days we had shared with the promenading holiday-makers on the sea-front the beckoning spectacle of Mull, a short handful of miles over from the esplanade, and rearing a backdrop which cut off farther views of the Isles. This is the view of Mull which gave it its name, a *Mull* being a promontory; and certainly the bulk of bens jostling into Scotland at this coast has little appearance of an island. To the north of this mass the mainland district of Morven pressed south, leaving between itself and the huge island the narrow sea-channel of the Sound of Mull. Through here lay our route, first of all to Tobermory, and the other townships of Mull, and then westwards beyond Ardnamurchan Point to the Small Isles. Once out of Oban, we hoped to avoid setting foot again on the mainland for some weeks at least.

We could expect trouble at the entrance to the Sound, where the island of Lismore chokes the channel and presses the tides into disturbances. We had sailed through here in the Hebridean cargo steamers, and had watched them reel a point or two off their course in the kick of the tide stream. A straight passage from north of Kerrera Island would lead us past Duart into the open Sound of Mull. We readily advised ourselves against this venture. The worst part of the tide race sets up in the half-mile channel between Lismore Lighthouse and the Lady Rock, but the disturbance trails off well to the south of that gap, and we felt our arrival in Mull might be more comfortable if we were to give this spot a respectable offing. The day was breezy enough, but in gusts, and our plan was to canoe round the north of Kerrera and half-way down its west coast, making from there a straight dart over to Loch Don in Mull and then round into the Sound by the Duart promontory.

There was a blizzard of rain as we came into the shore of Kerrera, and we huddled against the limpets of a low rock, delaying as long as we could the cold trickles that searched our bodies. The first wetting of the day was always the worst, whether from sea-water or rain, and we often found it more comfortable to be soaked in the surf while launching. These

MAP B

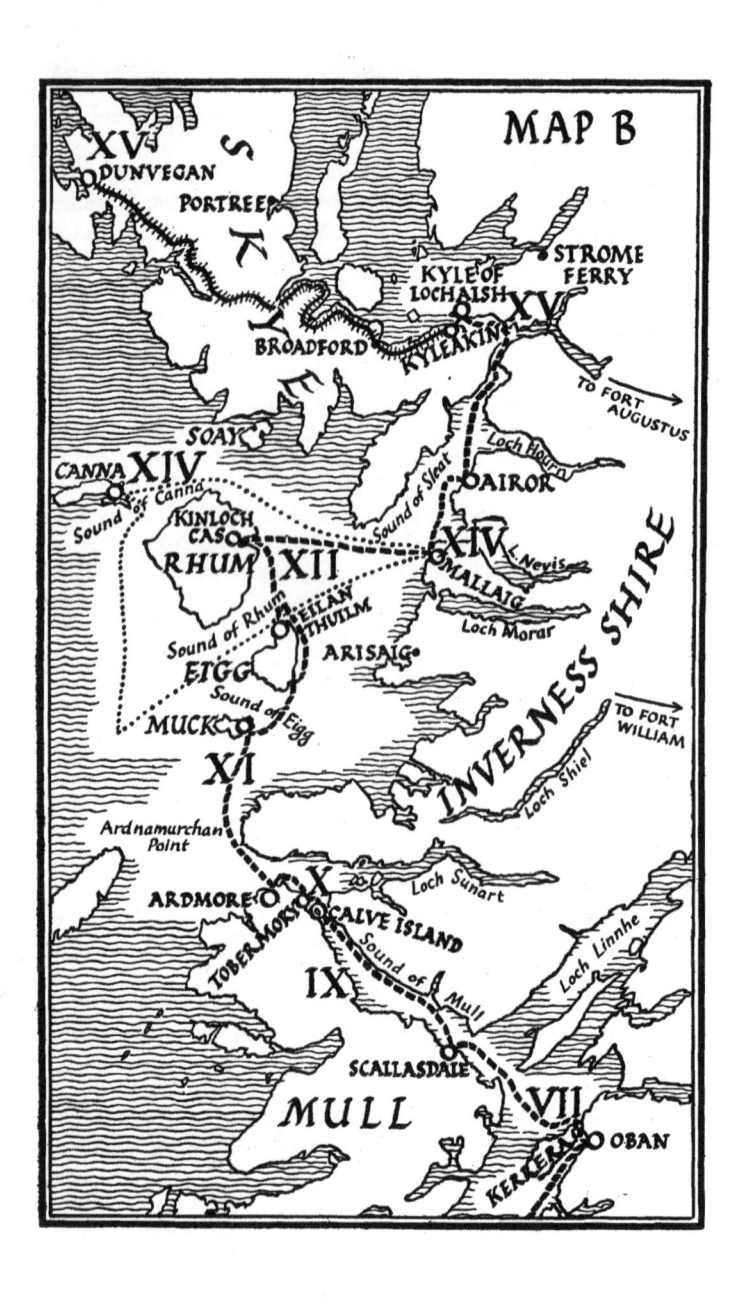

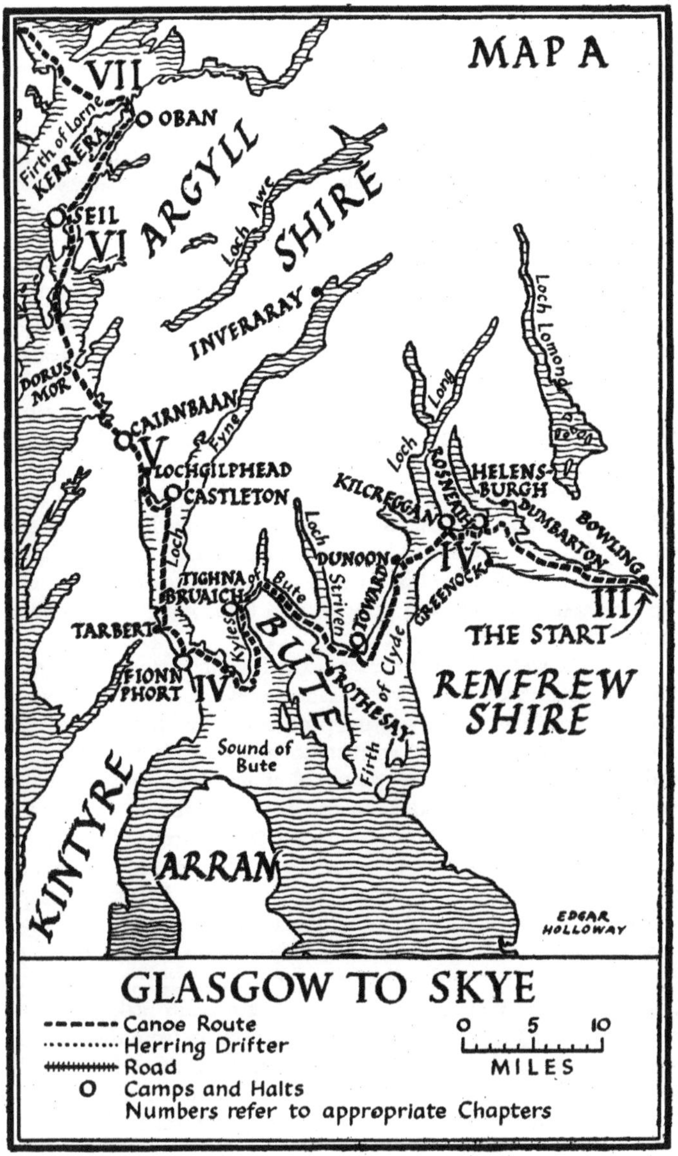
MAP A
VII
OBAN
Firth of Lorne
KERRERA
ARGYLL
SHIRE
Loch Awe
SEIL
VI
INVERARAY
Loch Lomond
DORUS MOR
CAIRNBAAN
Loch Fyne
V
LOCHGILPHEAD
CASTLETON
Loch Long
ROSNEATH
HELENS-BURGH
KILCREGGAN
DUMBARTON
BOWLING
Loch Striven
DUNOON
IV
TOWARD
Loch
TIGHNA BRUAICH
Kyles of Bute
GREENOCK
III
THE START
TARBERT
FIONN PHORT
IV
BUTE
ROTHESAY
Firth of Clyde
RENFREW SHIRE
Sound of Bute
KINTYRE
ARRAN
EDGAR HOLLOWAY
GLASGOW TO SKYE
Canoe Route
Herring Drifter
Road
Camps and Halts
Numbers refer to appropriate Chapters
0 5 10
MILES

rain squalls were with us constantly on that day, and we grew familiar with them, distrusting them only for the wind they signalled.

We were in no hurry to clear the point of Kerrera, as we were hoping to catch the value of a tide which had scarcely begun. It would have been better to take our passage in the slack water between tides, but that was a piece of local navigational lore we were about to learn for ourselves. In the meantime it was pleasant to share the low weedy rocks with the rain plowtering among reefs from which the charts warn real boats frantically. We landed and climbed the channel beacon—a juvenile impulse which I preserve unimpaired despite the passing of the years. So we splashed a trippery way round the shore and southwards to leave the Lady Rock area behind. On this western shore of Kerrera we were more exposed to the periodic blashing of the squalls, and the roundabout plan on which we had embarked began to appear a lengthy method of reaching Mull. At last we grew irritated at the rain wind which came like waves of infantry from the west, and lifted sea-water as well into our right ears; and we turned and faced into it straight for Mull, for the same reason as a Highland pony with a load will run up a hill instead of walking—to get it over quickly.

We got a wet and strenuous reward for our change of plans. For the first three miles we splashed onwards in brave style, gathering much water but making progress. And then we struck a great area of tide popple, with stationary waves which erupted and subsided in the same place, blowing their tops off like volcanoes, while the wind flung this chill lava about. Here we churned for a bleak two hours, making not a half-mile of progress in that time, until it seemed we were bewitched and would be here until we died, and that could not be long. This is a dreary sort of terror, to be caught struggling in waves which are going nowhere. Whether in the end we defeated this tidal race, or it moved from us, we raised our heads at the end of two hours to greet a more normal sea, in which we were again making some headway towards the Mull shore. We drove on from there until we almost grounded on Mull, determined to shake off the tidal heave. There we moored ourselves by holding to the floating blisters of bladder-wrack while we baled, and ate bannocks to celebrate our actual coming to the Isles.

It was a sheltered shore, and pleasant when we paddled on northwards. There is a lighthouse which is a memorial to William Black the novelist, much less a Victorian figure than he is now considered. On the corner of the point stood Duart Castle, seat of the chief of the MacLeans. It rose triumphantly from its ancient ruins only recently, because the determined previous chief made it his life's work to earn the money with which to rebuild. He did so, and lived in his new-born castle until he died there shortly before the war, aged over a hundred. That evening, as we rounded its promontory, the castle stood up for us proudly, and a man on the lawn, an undoubted MacLean, waved eagerly towards us in a salute of welcome. We had a brief thought for the symbolism of this Highland clan's resurgence in its own rights, by making battle successfully with the modern world, and we were bold to trace some distant parallel to our own vision of what might be in these places. A pleasant evening sun burst in to warm this thought, turning the world in a moment to a coloured delight.

Now we were in the Sound of Mull, close to the island's shore, and moving north-west along past some of the small hamlets in their bays, expecting to make our camp for the night at Scallasdale. This was a sheltered route, and our weather was now harmless, but mischievous. Past Duart, and another mile or two of rocky shore, Craignure Bay fell away to our left and opened up the wind to us. Tiny strong waves, packed together like plough furrows, rippled out of the bay. These were too close for us to ride. Each of them skelped us on the side of the hull, and flung up and into our faces, so that we were soon a-drip. Beyond the bay we hung cosily to the shore, among the reefs and well away from the navigable channel. This cheated the wind until we pushed in between the little Goat Skerries and rounded a small point to beach near the mouth of Scallasdale River.

It had been a troublesome day and we were glad to be on land. Although neither of us had been on this part of Mull before, we knew the feel of the island and this seemed a good place for us. The steep shore which fringed the waste of moor and rock led up to a small turf plateau above our heads. This looked like a splendid camp site, with a view through the Sound of Mull on both sides, from Lorne to Ardnamurchan. Distant scattered farm and croft houses seemed to promise the comforts of milk, eggs, and butter—possibly scones, and a yarn at night by a kitchen farm. It was a prospect which appealed to our chilled condition. And there was always the likelihood that some unexpected adventure would come, for that is the way in the islands.

So we grabbed the tent gear and scrambled up and over the edge of the plateau to our camping site. As we had expected, it was a glorious little stretch of turf. But we paused, for there were people on it, and something like a tall flagged lance planted and quivering medievally in the middle of it. Other distant figures were approaching. We sank down on the edge of the grass, feeling the inadequacy of our sodden rags, our holed sandshoes, our scratched and streaming legs. A man and a woman, standing a few yards from us, turned to stare, but politely, at what had emerged from the sea.

Before our vision settled, we had a glimpse of them as god-like creatures, their coloured garments made glorious by the evening sun; weapons in their hands and their youth dazzling.

We had disturbed them as they were holing out on the fifth green of a handsome golf course.

CHAPTER VIII

SEA CANOEING

The sea wants to know—not the size of your ship,
Nor built with what art;
Nor how big is your crew, nor your plans for the trip
—But how big is your heart.

THE modern kayak or decked canoe was first designed in the eighteen-sixties, by an energetic Christian called John MacGregor. He adapted the design from the craft used for open-sea work by primitive peoples on the edge of the Arctic, clothed its framework with rigid planking instead of skins, worked tirelessly to devise handy suits of sails, and called the craft *Rob Roy* after the most dashing member of his clan.

In a succession of *Rob Roy's*, MacGregor canoed through most of the rivers and lakes and along most of the coasts of Europe, leaving excitement and an outbreak of canoe clubs in his wake. The books he published about his trips are still the wisest and the most adventurous of their kind. With the coming of the small power-boat, canoeing fell into a decline, until the *Rob Roy* design was rediscovered, and eventually made portable by folding its hull, in a great enthusiasm for canoeing which took place in Germany between the wars.

Boat designing and building is still one of the personal fine arts. A ship of any size can have no personality unless she is built as an individual, conceived in her own right on the drawing-board and built from the keel up as a separate thing. It is always interesting to note the prejudice which exists in the Clyde area against mass production of ships, and the insistence, in that laboratory of skill, upon the creation of a new ship for each new job or purpose. The motor-car industry, for example, by the simplifying of its production into a mere factory task, has stultified its own technical development, although it has fulfilled its economic destiny.

Sailing, or any form of boat-work which does not depend on engine-power, has become largely a leisure occupation, and has therefore been able to remain personal. Occasionally there appears in this world of uncommercial boat-work a genius able to combine the skills of the sailor and the designer. MacGregor was one. Slocum and Uffa Fox are other undoubted names in this list. John Marshall had the gift, and would have gone far. To read the writings of the first three is to hear a blueprint think.

MacGregor held to the belief in his successive designs that a canoe should be built actually to fit the owner, like a suit of clothes. The standard of canoe-building has probably dropped since his day, when enthusiasts were forced not only to be their own designers, copying and adapting the best models, but often their own builders. MacGregor's story is one of unremitting supervision of the firms who produced all his gear, and he records bitterly, naming the firms concerned, that not one of them (in that age of craftsmanship) did the jobs properly.

We were spending so much of each day in the canoes that we had to study, at the outset, methods of doing our travelling in reasonable comfort. We anticipated that, to begin with, our hands would blister badly with the ceaseless paddling, and among the items in our departure equipment had been light skin gloves. The genteel gestures which accompany the drawing on of gloves caused laughter among spectators at Bowling and other points along the route. But by the time the gloves had worn and fallen off our hands in strips, the hands themselves were as hard as the paddles and the gloves were no longer needed.

This proved to be the case also with our inflated cushions, which we had thought should be inserted between ourselves and the bare floorboards. When inflated they perched us too high, and wobbling, and disturbed the balance of the canoes, apart from greatly reducing our paddling thrust. By the time we learned that the most efficient seat was on the firm floorboards themselves at keel height, with the cushions completely deflated to act as a flat thin mat of rubber, we had hardened appropriately to find this arrangement comfortable. On later occasions, while waiting to harden on a new trip, we found that the best temporary seat was a flat rubber kneeling-mat as used by floor-washers.

For clothes we wore only singlets and shorts, with our zipper jackets on very cold days. When launching away off a beach we wore canvas shoes. These came off once we were afloat and were wedged in below the stranding wire on the deck of the after-section. Coming in to shore again, we could get at them easily and pull them on, so that our feet were not too sorely battered by the stones as we got out to run the unmanned canoes clear up the beach.

Travelling in a canoe among our coastal waters can be done only by the grace of the tide and the wind. One lives and moves in a constant awareness of these mighty natural forces, and is engaged always in studying how to engage them as allies, rather than to encounter them in conflict. On our west coast, when the tide is flowing (that is, when it is 'coming in'), the stream of water moves north. When it ebbs, the water runs south again, draining off towards the Equator. High water is about six and a half hours before and after low water, so that the tide is full 'in' and full 'out' twice in every twenty-six hours or so. For an hour or two around high water, on either side of the precise moment when the tide 'turns' and starts to ebb, there is a period when it is doing nothing very definite, and the tidal movement in a stretch of sea, or even in a narrow channel, is hardly perceptible. There is a similar period of 'slack' water at the bottom of the ebb.

These conditions have all sorts of local variations, caused by the shape of the coast, and the sea-bed, and a great complication of other factors. So well, however, have our coasts been surveyed, and the surveys constantly revised, that most of the smallest local vagaries are known and recorded in the nautical almanacks, Admiralty and other official navigational publications, as well as in the useful little tide-tables handed out by the yachting firms. By a ready-reckoner system laid out as simply as the multiplication table on the back cover of the old Shorter Catechism, you can find out the time of high water at any village, harbour, or prominent navigation point on the coast.

In addition, the detailed charts of the coast are sprinkled with information and warning advice, particularly about any unorthodox set of the tide. Where a channel does not run clearly north and south, the flood-tide coming up from the south must go in to the channel by the handiest entrance it can find, and go out by the other. A novice navigator may not have the experience to tell from the other conditions present whether the flood stream will arrive from the east or the west. Do not let him worry. Sailormen have been here before; the information has been gathered and noted down in the charts and sailing directions.

Broadly, however, the flood-tide flows north, and the ebb-tide south, and if you are going north you will go when the tide does. According to the district, this will mean a stream running at from one to several knots in your favour. With a canoe, you have to adjust your entire time-table to that of the tide, and if the stream starts flowing an hour before dawn, you will require to be up in time to go with it, and so enjoy six hours or so of positive travel —a good day—before it turns against you. You can also travel in the short period of slack water, and also, of course, against the tide, if you must move on, but this will cut your pace considerably. Anything above three knots will be very tough work, while there are certain main coastal channels where the tide runs faster than you paddle. These tide factors scarcely affect power-boats or even the larger sailing yachts with auxiliary engines, but the canoeist's first lesson is to learn to be friendly with the tide.

And with the wind. Unlike the boat of normal design—even the rowing-boat—a canoe has little grip of the water. Only a few inches are below the surface, and the rest of the hull, with the figure of the canoeist, offers to the wind what is in effect a large proportional sail area. A wind on the water can blow a canoe before it like an inflated bladder. On our coasts the wind blows almost constantly. It is true that, in a sultry summer, calms may occur, but these are rare. During the three months of our trip we never happened to be afloat on a calm day.

The wind, which is the heart of the weather, is largely unpredictable. It has wild, unexpected local variations, and may squall and whisper its way round the compass in a few hours. Here it differs from the tide, which has at least a regular rhythm, although it held fast to the long-term secrets of its predictability until Lord Kelvin unlocked these only a little time ago. The best meteorologist I know is certain that the wind and its weather have a purpose predictable in terms of scientific practice: that it will, perhaps in our own time, be possible to display the rule by which the wind is made, saying where it will blow, and for how long, a week on Tuesday. And what will happen to the sailorman then?

A canoe may be paddled against a head wind, but it is work.

6. EASDALE SEEN FROM DUN MOR ON SEIL

Easdale is an island famous for its slate quarries, leased by a commune of workmen in the last century and run as a co-operative enterprise. Lunga and Scarba islands are in the distance.

7. SEUMAS AT STORNOWAY. *This canoe carried him across the Minch on his own in the year after our trip. It is a later model than the one shown below.*

8. PACKING UP A CANOE. *The late John Marshall, the builder of these boats which carried us to Skye, has just picked up one bulkhead on the right. Seamus, on the left, is about to unship the other one. This picture comes from Marshall's 'Canoes and Canoeing.'*

SEA CANOEING

The cunning voyager about to make an open-water passage prefers to wait until the wind is favourable. A favourable wind is one which is going his way, although he may have to be content with one which does not blow farther ahead than either quarter. A beam wind or anything ahead of that will bring up the muscle and cut down the rate of travel. Square sails, such as we used, blossom in a following wind. A fore-and-aft rig requires more elaborate gear, and is better with some drop-keel device to reduce leeway, or sideways skidding down the wind.

There is a good deal of fun still to be had by some suitably tough group prepared to investigate the whole range of canoe-sailing possibilities. John Marshall used to experiment in the Firth of Forth with a box-kite flying aloft and attached to his bow. To follow up this inspiration alone should ensure a release from boredom, and if its problems of remote control were to be overcome, the sea-canoeist could look forward to going with the wind, and at the wind's speed.

These two, tide and wind, are the chief allies, and they should both be on your side. With the wind and the tide in your favour there's nothing to stop you. Complications follow when the wind and the tide are opposed. This conflict sets up a difficult sea, and in open coastal water it may be the wet jabbly rhythmless sea which makes misery of travel. That is why, even on a good day with a steady wind blowing, two separate sets of sea conditions will be created—one when the tide is with the wind, and one when the tide turns against the wind.

Whatever tricks he may be up to in the rigging of sails, the main propulsion used by the canoeist will be his own paddling effort. The chief glory of the canoe is the extreme comfort of the rowing position. One faces forward, in an armchair, and sees all that is coming. The paddling action is a leverage between the two hands, and a feathering motion set by a quick wrist movement in the brief moment when neither paddle blade is in the water. The tendency when learning to paddle is to spread the hands too widely apart as they grip the shaft between the blades. With familiarity they come closer together. The novice also feels that the total length of the paddle is too little. This awkwardness, too, will pass, although few will be comfortable with a paddle of seven feet or less, the Eskimo length.

With practice the canoe keeps a much straighter course than

would seem possible from a merely mechanical examination of the side thrusts which create the movement.

This paddling is very much simpler than rowing. Results can be achieved from the first stroke, as we found with quite young children and with elderly non-seamen. There is no catching of crabs, losing rowlocks, and falling over backwards. Even the timid beginner feels happy while dipping gingerly and awaiting results. It is perhaps relevant to mention that the action reduces the waistline noticeably and puts bulk and hardness on to the upper parts. At the end of our trip we had each added fourteen or sixteen pounds of weight, all of it hard stuff round the shoulders; and we could almost span our waists with our hands.

We found that the subtle paddling leverages employed by all parts of the body could be assisted. A firm purchase was needed between the soles of our feet and the forward bulkheads. This was filled by the bundle of our sleeping clothes, tightly rolled and waterproofed into a firm cylinder on which our bare feet rested. A similar bundle with our change of clothes was braced in each canoe between the stern bulkhead and the small of our backs. We learned in our daily packing to calculate the diameter of these bundles to a fraction of an inch, so that we were aware of an easy leverage from toes to hips, and a slight stiffening of the physical tension gave us, when necessary, quick extra power in our paddle strokes. This was undoubtedly what MacGregor meant when he insisted that his canoes be made to the measurements of his own person.

A sustained feeling of grip and fit is of high importance in sea-canoeing. Much practice will bring experience to meet in comfort any of the great variety of wave and wind conditions, but from the start it is well to know that canoeing of this kind is a single art. The canoeist is, in fact, riding the canoe. Braced to hold it to him, and actually to wield it as a weapon of battle with the sea, he will learn how to lift it, and when, at the approaching waves. He must be as conscious of riding as a cyclist. With a beam-breaking sea, for example, there is a trailing of the lee paddle and then a sudden thrust and lift with it; at the same time the haunches give a flick of the canoe towards the wave, with precisely the movement used by a Hawaian maiden to swing her grass skirt.

Two people in one canoe will be very expert indeed if they can do this with perfect timing together. Most of the canoeing accidents happen in double-seater canoes which are neither big enough to be boats nor small enough to be solo weapons. We became convinced that the single-seater canoe is altogether safer, and makes this wave jousting most joyous. Whatever the excellence of the folding boat, many of which we tried, it would seem certain that the best canoe for sea and shore work is a rigid model, with some keel protection for the fabric.

Each craft should have its own safety margin. We felt doubly provided for with our rubber-tyre lifebelts and the sealed bulkheads. The canoes could remain afloat with the centre section completely waterlogged, while if we lost them altogether the lifebelts would have been a solace. We never had to resort to the latter test, but the tyres were comforting. A sea-canoe must carry its own buoyancy. The water cannot be kept out except by seaming the canoeist to his craft by means of his garments, a dangerous practice in our beamier European canoes. If the hull is open from end to end without bulkheads, it can fill in a sea and be sunk. Inflated beach balls, or anything of the sort both light and airtight, should be stuffed into the bow and stern points and tests made to ensure that the filled canoe can still float in rough water bearing twice the canoeist's weight. A picturesque buoyancy device is the installation at each end of the hull of a sufficient quantity of table-tennis balls, penned in by a barrier of net.

Comfort, a word which has made several recent appearances in these pages, is admittedly only relative in its meaning. We rarely travelled dry, and it was normal for us to be sitting permanently in several inches of water. From time to time in our day's journey we would stop to bale this out. For this purpose we had cans, and sponges to mop up the last half-inch. Sitting on the extreme lowest part of the craft, one becomes aware of the slightest first intrusion of water, and so it is better to develop a familiarity—an attitude not difficult after the first chill tremors and trickles.

We grew to a similar state of mind in the matter of our canoeing clothes. These mere scraps we simply took off on landing and threw in a heap, knowing there was little chance of their being dry in the morning anyway. Saltwater-soaked clothing will not dry until it has been rinsed in fresh water, and we did not find it necessary to go to such elaborate lengths.

We found quickly, as we must, methods of packing which kept the rest of our equipment imperviously dry. Treble-wrapped in rubber groundsheets, oiled silk, and then heavy oilcloth, all bound like string bags, our bundles shared the swilling bilge-water with us, and never leaked. One separate bundle apiece contained our 'going ashore' outfits, along with a dry towel. On landing, we would heave the canoes up out of the sea's way, pick a camping site, and run the tent up. The going-ashore bundles were jerked open; our singlets and shorts cast aside. The towels flayed us up pinkly, and in seconds we would have thrown on shirt, kilt, jacket, bonnet, shoes and stockings, and be ready for visiting.

If the day was dark and chill when we arrived, making it necessary to postpone until the morning an excursion for provisions or conversation, we varied the routine by crawling with all our bundles into the tent, lacing the door, lighting both stoves, and sitting naked upon a blanket while steam rose from us in a most pleasing way. Only mounting hunger would drive us to stir from the luxurious dwam which this practice induced.

This may well be the proper place at which to say something of our food arrangements. We had two folding pressure stoves and a suitable outfit of light-weight utensils. The provisions we carried in waterproof bags, and very large bundles they made. Bread, we found, was not a suitable item of travelling provisions, unless for our midday sandwiches. It was bulky, and we could dispose of six loaves at frightening speed.

The basis of our eating was oatmeal, lentils, dried fruit and potatoes. We made quantities of lentil soup, or at least a pottage, boiling up steeped lentils into a fine green khaki mush into which we dropped, when we could spare it, a rasher of bacon by way of stock.

Oatmeal brose was the true foundation of the expedition, and the correct method of making it must be put on record. A quantity of coarse oatmeal—with salt 'to taste' as they say—is placed in a bowl and boiling water poured over it. The water must be boiling hard as it pours and there should be enough of it to just cover the oatmeal. A plate is immediately placed over the bowl like a lid. You now sit by for a few minutes, gloating.

This is your brose cooking in its own steam. During this pause, slip a nut of butter under the plate and into the brose. In four or five minutes whip off the lid, stir the mass violently together, splash in some milk, and eat. You will never again be happy with the wersh and fushionless silky slop which passes for porridge. This was the food whose devotees staggered the legions of Rome; broke the Norsemen; held the Border for five hundred years; and are standing fast on borders still. It is a dish for men. It also happens to taste superbly. We ate it twice a day, frequently without milk, although such a simplification demands what an Ayrshire farmer once described to me as a 'guid-gaun stomach'. He is a happy traveller who has with him a bag of oatmeal and a poke of salt. He will travel fast and far.

Dried fruit was a pleasant accompaniment. We always soaked a large canful overnight and stewed it briefly in the morning. The fruits could also be eaten in their dry wrinkled state, when determined mastication brought out juicy hints of their dormant virtues. At times we made pancakes, or even simpler articles with flour.

After breakfast each morning we prepared a prodigious bundle of food to be consumed *en route*. This consisted of sandwiches, which we shared by laying the canoes alongside each other wherever we might be. In seas too rough for the proximity, the man with the sandwiches would have to pass some over by paddle. This meant balancing the sandwiches on one of the blades, and holding the paddle out like an old-fashioned church collecting-ladle, until the other snatched the food off safely. Here again we grew skilful, and in the end the gestures of proferring and grabbing, among the heaving of the seas, canoes and paddle, were dainty indeed. A loaf or two, followed by some dried fruits, or a few hard-boiled eggs, were adequate and satisfying in these conditions. Strangely, although we carried bottles for drinking-water, and were many hours afloat at a stretch, we rarely felt thirsty on the sea.

CHAPTER IX

THE SPANISH ARMADA

>   They came no far and glamoured road,
>   They bear no magic sign;
>   What wisdom have they from abroad?
>   We ken their kin and line.
>   What folly to believe that they
>   Could profit us on market day!

IT is unusual to see a startled Highlander. Sudden exclamations of surprise form little part of his vocabulary. The words of ejaculation which he employs are vented only after consideration, and have a ponderable quality. The reason for this stoicism is that he is inured to the unexpected. It is indeed the constant accompaniment of his life, for there is a surprise round every Highland corner.

We had splashed ashore at Scallasdale expecting a deserted moorland bog, and we had found a golf course. As we watched them, ourselves like sodden kelpies, only more tousled, the man and the girl holed out levelly, nodded towards us with grave courtesy, and took their trim way to the next tee, leaving the lance of the fifth hole reared and swaying in possession of the field where we crouched. They drove off adequately—she with a trig yellow jumper and a swing like an angel—and walked away down the fairway out of our lives.

They dwindled, and we came back to the chill present. Dropping back to the beach, we stripped, dried, and changed before setting off to the farm of Scallasdale, nesting distantly in its rich woody garden on the far side of the course. Here would undoubtedly be a suitable camping corner, well beyond the range of the fashionable sporting scene we had just left.

In a field near the farm we encountered a large and sturdy bell-tent. A few skirmishes round it revealed that it was unoccupied. We learned at the farm that it was the property of a regular visitor to the place, Meg Buchanan, the actress, better known to Scots radio audiences as Mrs. McFlannel. Later we had to confess to her that we had moved in and squatted overnight in her tent, on the suggestion of the farm folk.

There can be times, concerning the elements of living—food and shelter—when a bell-tent pitched on wet grass can appear, in perspective, to offer the grossest of luxury. We hauled our gear into it, and weighted the canoes above the tide with stones from the beach. After the frail gauze of our lightweight, the bell-tent rolled sturdily through the rising wind like a battleship, flinging off the gouts of rain that struck her like streams of bullets. It was a comfortable might for the tent also, because our lit stoves cheered up the interior, and we trimmed her rigging afresh against Meg's return.

The Campbells of Scallasdale Farm received us warmly, and we sat in to tea with them and heard the news of the place. Apart from the onerous tasks of the farming and the crofts around there were ample activities to cheer their leisure time. Golf is a recent sport in the West Highlands; unlike the east of Scotland, where the game was born and has its roots. So the course was a new craze, taken up with great keenness. Everyone was playing golf, and used clubs and balls from relatives in other parts of the country were arriving to fire the zeal of the new recruits. Other active sports, dances, a badminton club, filled the winter, which is farming's holiday time.

Among the farm folk was a town lad in his teens, who had been working there for a year or two. 'I would never want to leave here,' he told us. 'Ye never weary; there's always something interesting going on.' In his words was a summary of much of the continuing and living significance of our Highlands. In this remote lively corner of Mull, they were a new proof of what we had come to prove.

Another was to be found in a little personal achievement of the son of the house. An old cottar building standing near had been 'restored' by the landowner, mainly for decorative purposes, and when it was to be roofed no professional thatcher could be found in the neighbourhood to do the job. All the recent house-building had been concerned with more modern forms of roofing. However, thatching was wanted, and thatching would be done. 'I'll try it myself,' said Duncan Campbell, and he set to, with someone carting the rushes to him. There was the finished task, as good a job of thatching as we saw in our whole journey, and a sign of the ready invention which exists beyond the range of chain-store life.

The Campbells showed us round their charming garden, pointing out, among their trees, the superb Spanish chestnut which was probably the largest in Scotland. They told us with a twinkle that local belief attributed the planting of the tree to survivors from the Spanish Armada.

Throughout the British Isles there is a range of legend which deals generously with the prowess of other nations. We have always been kind to the foreigner. This is an acute and comic development of a determined human belief, that no good thing can come out of the adjacent soil. For the Scottish scene the situation is neatly summed up in a recent incident, already classic. A visitor to a small town made conversation with a citizen about a young native of the place who was already an author of renown. 'Whit!' exclaimed the townsman, in a spasm of repudiation. '*Him* write books? I kent his faither!'

More than once we laughed irresistibly in the faces of certain holiday-makers who would come running to watch us land, with shouts of 'Hurrah! Here come the Danish canoeists!'—and were almost indignantly crestfallen to hear us talk. They had rushed to salute some noble and mysterious alien impulse, and remained to be critics of foolhardy locals.

History is a peculiarly rich vein for this attitude, since the topical proofs are not present. One will be told freely in Scotland, with chapter and verse, that the kilt was invented by an English navvy-master; that some London tailor was the first to devise tartans; that (although the sword and the pipes kept us alive as a nation) our greatest sword-maker was a central European, and the MacCrimmons, the master pipers, were Italians; that no one ever climbed Scottish peaks until some gentlemen came from Oxford in 1860 or thereabouts.

I do not believe these tales; and I disbelieve them by instinct, without the need for research. I have a habit of labelling them all with what is intended to be the sceptical title of 'Spanish Armada', because the Armada is by far the richest seam for the pro-foreigner school of historical study. One is deeply in the toils of it on all the Scottish islands, from the north of Shetland down to Gigha.

THE SPANISH ARMADA

The story is put forward that all our coasts are thickly peopled with descendants of Spaniards shipwrecked with the Armada, and that these introduced to the natives, not only a dominant racial type, but also a wealth of learning in the arts, husbandry, and the graces of life. 'The inhabitants of Barra are all Spanish' I was told, on the eve of my first visit to that truly Celtic Hebridean isle. 'The men are all olive-skinned, and they wear gold earrings.' Alas, but I never found a male earring, nor a native guitar, in all my visits: and the dark ones among them looked incorrigibly Celtic to me!

These Spanish castaways had many skills, if all the tales are even half true. They taught the women of Shetland and Fair Isle to knit, and those of Harris to weave. To other islands came cheese-makers, or sea-dogs skilled in fancy sewing and lace-making. The more masculine were meantime teaching the eager islanders how to distil whisky, build and navigate boats, breed ponies and dogs, improve their flocks, fields, and woods, and other useful arts which have not survived in Spain. Others devoted themselves to the design of buildings, the illumination of manuscripts, and the general raising of taste and standards. It can be seen that all progress and all knowledge were lacking in Scotland until that autumn of 1588 when the Spaniard was washed up.

History has done its best for England too. It is said that there are villages of Devon where the entire population is clearly of Spanish origin, descendants of refugees from the Armada. As if the men of Bideford, for their part in that affair, had need to improve their stock by a Latin importation.

Plenty of history has been written about the Armada, but the facts will hardly support the prowess with which the Spaniards are decorated at the scenes of their shipwrecks. It was a terrifying disaster which overtook them, the moment they entered the English Channel, and pursued them all round the British coasts. Seumas and I could even feel for their wretchedness, in that summer of our own, for 1588 was another of those incessant periods of storm, with winter gales swamping the whole autumn. Wounded and scattered by Drake, the Armada ships squeezed out of the Channel through the Straits of Dover and staggered north along the English east coast, with Howard chasing them beyond the Forth. On they heaved, the remnants of them, round the Orkneys and south past Scotland and Ireland to the open Atlantic and a long struggle back to home ports, successfully reached by only a battered few. Here and there on our west coast they crashed and vanished.

The picture of their alleged social influence suggests orderly and able bands of them marching ashore and setting to rights the long-neglected education of the natives. In contemporary eyes, they cut a different figure. James Melville, the minister of Anstruther, saw them. He describes in his Diary how one wandered galleon anchored off his town while the commander came ashore to beg for water and stores. It was a sharp moment for the Fifers, as, granting the favour, they thought of those of their own seafaring number who had died on the faggots of the Inquisition. There was nothing formidable about the ship's company of about two hundred and fifty 'for the maist part', says Melville, 'young beardless men, silly, trauchled and hungered'.

The most famous Armada ship in Scotland was not wrecked by storm, but blown up and sunk when at anchor in Tobermory Bay, in Mull. Fragments of salvage have been recovered from time to time, and the known presence of the wreck in shallow water, with the belief that it was in some way the treasure ship of the Armada, has made the spot for a century or two the scene of trial for all new diving equipment as it was invented. A gun recovered in a drag is believed to have been designed and cast by Benvenuto Cellini; but the most thrilling signal from the deep was experienced by the crew of a barque last century, who, weighing anchor, found a gold doubloon stuck by a dab of mud to one of the flukes. Many of this galleon's crew are believed to have been safely ashore when she went down, but there is no record that any of them settled in Mull. They probably set out to plod their way overland homewards like the other scattered survivors.

These were the fortunate ones, and there were very few of them. Of the twenty ships or less wrecked on the whole length of the Scottish and Irish coasts, not many men came ashore and lived. Over eleven hundred dead bodies came up on one Irish beach. Those who came in alive quickly joined them. One actually survived to creep trembling home to Spain and write his memoirs, telling of the terrible men of Ireland who came out of the shore bog to despatch and despoil his comrades. His narrative is

THE SPANISH ARMADA 83

given a mounting frenzy of terror by the recollection that these Irish were claiming to be brutally held down by the English, who had just scourged God's favourite Spaniards; while with his own eyes he had seen an Ireland which was under no man's law at all. There were certain survivors who got ashore also in England, but there is no historical doubt about their fate. Froude describes bluntly how the officers were imprisoned for the ransom they might fetch, while all the others rescued were shot or hanged on the spot.

So that the Spanish Armada has left nothing more real than a tourist tale; although, in the unbalanced narrative of the West and its life, that can be real enough. But until an island is discovered where the men are called largely Pedro and Juan, and the people speak a Hispano-Gaelic tongue and drink their whisky from *porrons*, one will be able to assume that the folk of the Hebrides who happen to bear the dark complexion of their forebears belong to a Scottish race which was in its place before the Spaniard was in his.

Not that the Armada was an unalloyed victory for England and her neighbours. Indeed, it is clear to me that the Spaniards got the last word, although I have not seen the point made before. These months in the middle of 1588 were summer turned winter, with week-long gales constantly renewed. 'No one remembers such a season', said the Duke of Medina Sidonia, Commander of the Armada, writing to his king. Nor did he and the other survivors spare themselves in describing the weather, for it was one way of assuaging the disaster. For long after, the human stragglers were landed by neutral ships on the coasts of the Baltic and the Low Countries. And as they lurched their way home, gaunt and shaken, displaying their rock-scarred wounds gouged by early frost-bite, they planted in Europe for ever the grim legend of the British climate.

Many of the people at Scallasdale came to see our canoes. We gave solo trips to all who wanted them, and could readily have set up a profitable hiring business on the shore—an opportunity which was to arise frequently. It was not a bad day when we left eventually, in the afternoon. The wind was less than moderate, and diminishing slowly. Heading for Tobermory we had showers of rain for most of the way, but these are little-noticed discomforts once the boats are fairly launched and dampness is familiar. We took as straight a line as possible for the bay of Tobermory, seventeen miles away; a course which carried us well across to the Morven shore opposite the village and bay of Salen.

This very patch of water in the two-mile broad channel is the opening scene of Scott's 'Lord of the Isles'. The whole first part of the poem reads like a gazetteer of the Sound of Mull. Our nearest mainland was the Point of Ardtornish with its ruin of castle, once the splendid seat of the Lords, whose minstrels are discovered singing up the curtain in Scott's opening scene.

In its day, this great castle had been the gathering place and parliament of the chiefs of the Isles, and it is said that Edward I of England met them here in a fifth-column assembly to enlist them as allies in his mortal battle with the mainland Scots. Drawing a long and picturesque bow, Scott describes how Robert and Edward Bruce, homeward bound from Rathlin on the task of winning back Scotland, bring their small foundering ship into Ardtornish Bay and become involved in the wedding celebrations of the Maid of Lorne. In the meantime Lord Ronald's galleys go past, with a following wind and heaving an even faster course with their thousand oars, showing off before the bride. All four settings of that crammed opening narrative—the Maid's rooms, the minstrels' hall, the MacDonald armada, the ill-found Bruce ship, with the wind and the rending sails, the well-fed magnificent islesmen on their rowing benches, the harping, the Maid's tears—they go cutting into one another like a well-edited film. It may be old-fashioned stuff, but, by the Lord! it moves and slashes. We are all, to paraphrase Stevenson, very clever fellows nowadays, but we cannot tell stories like Walter Scott.

The Sound of Mull, with its villages and castles, is now less peopled. At the end of last century, Morven, the lovely land which forms the north of the Sound, had less than a third of the population with which it started the century. From the water, the whole visible land below the mountains is corded with old run-rigs, showing where many people have been. Cultivated patches are now rare, and the old homesteads have crumbled into the bracken on land which, at its present best, is only rough grazing for sheep.

Where have they gone, the people who were here? Mull has had the same decline in numbers. The figures of the first post-war census (1948) showed Mull's present population to be

THE SPANISH ARMADA 85

less than a quarter of what it was in 1811. For every nine people who lived in Mull at the beginning of last century, there are only two to-day. It is a terrifying deprivation, and we shall be looking at it more closely again.

There are ways of measuring a population which are more revealing than a mere count of heads. A brief survey by means of telephone directories is, I believe, more pointed than one dealing with census returns. The telephone is, of course, not essential to the life of a community, but it is one modern way of assessing a social and active citizenship.

Mull is the home of the MacLeans. They were never a numerous clan, although they had five hundred men out in the 'Forty-five'. Here, and on some of the adjacent islets and coast fringes, is the cradle of the clan, the source of them all. On the whole island of Mull there are only ten MacLeans on the telephone. There is one more in Buenos Aires, where eleven MacLeans have telephones. London has, in round figures, 220 phoning Mac-Leans, and Glasgow a hundred more than London. There are 280 in Chicago, and in Manhattan—an island about the size of Colonsay which happens to contain the City of New York—115. Toronto with 370 has more MacLeans on the telephone than Glasgow. Vancouver has 200, and Calgary, the town in Alberta which was christened by those who went from the village of that name in Mull, has 65. In Dunedin, New Zealand, there are 30. What a scattering is here! In a world hook-up, the ten MacLean subscribers in Durban, South Africa, could absorb the entire telephone strength of the clan in the island they all belong to. It would be difficult to guess at the world population of the MacLeans, although I see no difficulty, and a great deal of joy, in a new numbering of the tribes, if it were to be carried out by all the clans.

In the meantime I will say, for the MacLeans, that while they have been scattered, they have obviously not been lost. There is hardly one of these sundered MacLeans, and the other clansmen, but will be often busy deaving his own coterie with claims of proud ancestry. Here is a great, warm, loyal network of family about the world, ready to be drawn imaginatively together, and that for good.

Late in the evening, we were drawing in close along the Mull shore, where the Aros woods were hanging heavily. There were no special incidents in the afternoon's travel. We were jumbled from time to time among the conflicting tides which are the characteristic of the Sound of Mull. Scott mentions them, with the eye of a hillman noting another element, and they must have been heavily impressed upon him by the seamen who took him on his Western Isles trip.

The bay of Tobermory is almost landlocked by Calve Island, to the north of which is the main entrance to the bay. The south-west flank of the island makes a long narrow strait with Mull, and it was for this channel we headed, while the houses and spires of Tobermory, so familiar to us from previous cargo-boat visits, became more and more distinct ahead. A shoreward wind helped us here, and we got the sails up. Then we were in the canal-like strait, with the bay opening out ahead. Calve Island is an entire farm, and one of the girls was driving in the cows, which kept pace with us along the shore as we paddled. The family came out in front of the farm-house to wave us past.

The last mile of open water was across Tobermory Bay, where cargo puffers were at anchor, waiting for the next tide for their passage round Ardnamurchan Point. The tide was at its height, and all the shore of the bay was covered, the sea reaching high up the sea-wall. First we steered for the Old Pier. As its dark brown stones approached, we were aware of a frieze of onlookers which thickened at the pierhead, watching towards us, while many others bobbed along the front street and ran down the pier to join those at the end. Soon we were at fifty yards distance, and a generous applause was set up. It was a particularly self-conscious moment. We dug the bay with our blades, much bedraggled and tired, while a hand-clapping crackled like a growing furze-fire, and the children gave shrill cheers.

Shorewards, we heard repeated frequently for the first time the shouted joint nickname by which we were known throughout the Islands from that time forward: 'The Canoe Boys! . . . It's the Canoe Boys!'—and the shop doors became crowded and windows went up. We headed over to our left, where the river, surging full after the rain, spread out in a high little delta and promised a patch of shore. Before we came to ground, and stepped over the side, the throng was round to meet us, and the younger ones were already waiting ankle-deep in the shallows to pull us in. Dozens of hands of all sizes palmed and supported the canoes as we lifted them up. There was a great assembly present by the time this was done, so that we could have held a meeting there and then.

Through the crowd came pressing the tall figure of Kenneth Macfarlane, the grocer, general merchant, and newspaper correspondent, who took the situation into his versatile hands. He greeted us with a kind courtesy, putting only a few needful questions about where we had come from that day and when we might be leaving. It was as near to a civic welcome as we achieved; then—

'Are you looking for rooms or a hotel?'

'No—we're camping.'

'All right! You, Angus'—and he enlisted a boy—'show these gentlemen up to . . .'—and he described a camp site near by. 'You other boys, carry the rest of the things!'—and to us—'They'll show you where to go. It's in the wood near the power-house, just up at the back there. I'll get a wee paragraph off to the papers telling them you've arrived. You'll likely be sending off your own stories in the morning. Give me a look in at the shop when you're passing. The canoes will be safe here.'

There was no more than that. In three minutes after landing the canoes were empty on the shore, surrounded by spectators, and intact in the protection of an unseen authority. We were on our way up the road by the river, each man carrying nothing but his oar over his shoulder, padding inland like Homer's mariner, in the wake of a line of small native bearers.

We slept that night, and for some nights to come, in a sweet grassy clearing perched a few yards above the main road to Salen and Craignure, and out of sight of all passers-by. We could lie with the morning light watery on the canvas roof, and watch through the open door as the morning steamer clanked off from the pier to make for Oban. The steep gravel pitch up a little cliff face towards the plateau came to be as well known as home, and we could find our way aloft in the black darkness without a handhold, coming up from the lighted main street not fifty yards away.

In spite of its rollicking name, Tobermory has a gentle connotation. The name means 'Mary's Well', and the fine bay has certainly been a refuge and a shorefall for mariners since men have taken to the waters. Like Tarbert, it is a natural building site. Any township following the normal contours of such a ground plan could hardly be ill-built. In its present shape Tobermory is the result of a bold piece of eighteenth-century planning, when the British Fisheries Society settled on this place and on Ullapool, another handsome grouping of homes, hotels and shore, as the two main centres of the herring industry. By a typical twist of Highland industrial caprice, Tobermory has no contact with the present herring industry.

Of less than a thousand inhabitants, it is nevertheless the largest 'town' and the economic centre of Mull. Tourists and holiday-makers are its main business. Its port is the chief outlet for such agricultural produce as the island has to export, and its shops serve a large hinterland. In these shops one can buy, in fair times, not only the enormous proprietary range of present-day groceries, but Coll cheese, early potatoes from Barra and Treshnish, carrots from Muck, salted herrings cured in Ardnamurchan, salt cod, ling sun-dried on the rocks, honey and gooseberries from Mull itself, and all the rest.

The only consistent row of houses in sight from the bay is the shore range of tenements. The other dwellings are perched here and there on the cliff ledges, stepping up to the skyline, which is dominated by the mass of the Western Isles Hotel, suspended above the pier. One can climb inland and find, on plateaux, streets of whitewashed cottages like fisher rows. But there are, of course, no fishers.

With its hotels and boarding-houses, bus tours, boat and car hires, inland fishing, golf course, and a list of attractions, Tobermory has groomed itself efficiently for a career of tourism. What delighted us most about the place at that time was its recently completed and self-contained hydro-electric scheme. The river running down into the bay had been dammed, and a tiny powerhouse erected where a water-flywheel flew and hummed incessantly. This project had been faced and accomplished by a small burgh of only a few hundred citizens. The civic promotion committee had been astounded and warmly encouraged by the response of the inhabitants, as almost every household in the place installed electricity, although the capital outlays had made necessary a very high initial charge per unit. All the

9. BACK OF KEPPOCH, NEAR ARISAIG. *Hens, arable fenced against grazing cattle, a fishing boat on the shore—such is the crofters' economy. Skye is in the background beyond the Sound of Sleat.*

10. CALVE ISLAND. *This view from above Tobermory shows wooded Aros in Mull on the right, and the mainland hills of Morven away on the left. The farmhouse is over the lowest point of the horizon of Calve Island.*

11. HEBRIDEANS. *Hundreds took trips under their own power.*

appropriate gadgets were also installed—irons, fires, hair-driers, vacuums, bed-lights—and the community at one bound moved from paraffin lamps to electricity, having never known the use of gaslight.

The most common criticism made of the Highlander is that his character is unyieldingly conservative, refusing to change. He is certainly, on his home ground, a slow starter in method, but rarely in the acceptance of amenity. Since the war the Tobermory scheme has come under the wider powers of the North of Scotland Hydro-Electric Board, but at the time it was constructed the supply was a gallant and lonely triumph.

We stayed long enough in Tobermory to become almost citizens. It was a good place in which to see in operation most of the factors which create the Highland Problem. It was also a good place to be. In a few days we had produced and sold several weighty feature articles, and it did appear that we were being sought as, in some way, authorities on these endless themes. A judicious hint of canoeing thrills and dangers spiced some of these writings; in other cases we found that the main topic alone was sufficient; that there appeared to be a public in Scotland interested in these concerns. This is less of a novelty now, but at the time it was difficult to prise open a market for new facts on old worries.

We were able to take time to pause. The publishing of the articles brought in more information and controversy. We were stopped in the street and offered themes. Occasionally a voice, wise in pessimism, would deny all hope, and we would hear a recital such as this: schemes had been tried before for the development of Highland resources; they had failed. They would always fail. The place was done. The young people wouldn't stay. What was the good of scraping a living here when there were jobs to be had in Glasgow and Canada (the twin El Dorados!). The soil was too poor for crops. The weather was hopeless, anyway. We would find that out fast enough! For one thing, we would never get round Ardnamurchan Point. . . . All this was to apply, with a note of personal resentment at our intrusion, the theme of 'It's too late in the year!' to our mission as well as to our trip. These acerbities were rare, and came only from those very few whose patience had utterly broken down: or others who, having tasted of the sponge dipped in vinegar which is constantly presented to the Highland mouth, admitted to their agreement only those who would take a portion of their despair.

For the rest, Tobermory was overwhelmingly kindly and keen. There was a great run on the canoes, most of Tobermory at one time or another, young and old, having a trip aboard under solo power. Provost McGilp, the banker whose hobby was the buying and selling of farm stock, gave frequent displays of the dash he brought to the civic chair when he paddled round the bay, with a flock of rowing-boats manned by the youngsters in train. Once a destroyer of the Royal Navy anchored in the bay, and the exuberant Provost requisitioned one of the canoes, instead of the official launch, in which to pay his courtesy visit. He returned for the launch with a rueful grin. On reaching the destroyer he had paddled all round her, hailing the smart figures on deck and announcing himself, with a request for a companion-ladder. But the Navy would have none of him. They simply ignored his irresponsible person, although they plainly heard and saw him. He had to paddle to the shore and return by the orthodox method. Now he knows why they call it the Silent Service.

At dances in the Aros Hall, or by visits to the island, we fell in more and more with the MacDonalds of Calve. This island, the half-closed gate across Tobermory Bay, was a single-family farm, and we felt greatly drawn to the young people who were running it—not only because of their gay company, but because their household was a microcosm of the Highland Problem. We spent some days with them, working at their hay harvest, and paddling back to Tobermory long after dark, when even the town lights were out and only a few lamps, and the red fixed light on the pier, showed us the way ashore.

Soon, one day, we struck our camp above the power-house, loaded up, and paddled with all our goods over to Calve. There we pitched camp near the house, on a green above the shore, and worked at farming.

CHAPTER X

FAMILY FARM

> No season's winds impair her,
> The gentle flower that grows
> Deep root—like they who wear her—
> Strong on the shores that bear her,
> Our wild and lovely rose.

THE Atlantic fences Calve on all sides. The whole island is a single farm of less than two hundred acres, with a good proportion of arable to rough grazing. Blackfaced sheep cropped right to the edge of the seaweed, and in the spring there was an extra task of shepherding to be done with a constant patrol of the shore rocks, where the unsteady new lambs often fell and got wedged, or dropped into the sea. Once, during a south-easterly gale, Janet jumped in after a week-old lamb which had lost its footing and was swimming feebly in the wrong direction. She was over the shoulders in the chopping breakers before she caught up with him and bore him to the shore.

The Calve sheep and cattle soon lost their young curiosity and gave up investigating the nature of the sea. The dairy cows lived well off the salty grass, and we were at the cutting of ample hay for their winter needs. The hens scraped unobtrusively, and the ducks led their small flotillas up and down the strait of water which parts Calve from Mull. The sheep-dogs, instead of patrolling the usual farm road on the wait for strangers, barked any arrivals in to land at the jetty. They were sheep-dogs only, for the herding of the cows was the exclusive duty of a proud little Cairn bitch, who 'speaks only Gaelic', as we were told when we met her first. She had an insistent yap, but she reserved it for the cows, and for the collies who dared to intervene in her employment. There was a bull, and three horses.

One other creature on the domestic roll of the farm was an unseen, referred to as 'Miss Campbell', for whom steaming heaps of food were frequently carried behind the byre. We heard of her first when scraps and potato-peelings were being piled up after dinner. 'That's for Miss Campbell', we were told without a twinkle; and when we failed to understand, the thing ceased to be the reference of normal usage and became a jest for them again, after years of use and wont. We tried to guess, and failed, not knowing that 'Miss Campbell' had quotation marks round her name. At last we were allowed to carry her pail, and were led merrily to meet her, behind the byre, to where her wet flat nose snuffled eagerly at the lintel of her sty door.

She was the pig which they fattened annually. It had been many years since the name had been invented for the first of a series of these yearly residents, and the jest had quietened to a normal household mention, until our enquiring had revived it. No rancour was in the baptism, but a sufficient historical awareness. There was no need for either of us to comment or demur. This was a MacDonald farm!

And the folk? The gracious matriarch of this home was Mrs. MacDonald, already widowed some years since, but a happy woman, as well she might be with her gay household about her. Of her large family, four still remained at home. Donald, the eldest, and Malcolm; and the two youngest girls, Janet and Margaret. All his life Donald had been delicate; quiet among his robust clan, a gentle spectator on the edge of their ploys. The main work of the farm fell on the mighty shoulders of Malcolm—'Calum' to us all, with the power and patience to be a good farmer. We were with him late in the autumn, after our trip, when the corn was cutting, and for two days he coaxed and gentled a young new horse to take his share in the reaper harness. This task of infinite kindness and understanding is called, foolishly, 'breaking' a horse.

We did not see, but we heard about, the occasion when he put the ring in the bull's nose. It is a gruesome short operation without anæsthetic, requiring a preliminary driving of a sharpened skewer through the tender gristle of the bone below the nostrils. Compared with this, ordinary bull-fighting by a toreador may well appear like a soft afternoon of dawdling. Although the others of the family all worked, and heavily, at every outside farm task, Calum did not summon any of them to assist in this one. Indeed, he did not tell them that it was afoot. He simply rounded up the bull, a vicious Ayrshire, hitched him to the stoutest beam on the island, and ringed him single-handed. The bull's demeanour whenever Calum was in view showed that he had never forgotten this mastery. Calum was also strong in an athletic way. We used to pitch a stone in the evenings. By now Seumas and I were not frail, but Calum could putt yards beyond our best. At the Tobermory Games he could always get into the prize list, even among the circus of professional athletes who tour these events.

To Janet and Margaret went all the domestic work of the house, and the feeding of the smaller animals like hens, ducks, the pig, calves, sick lambs, dogs, cats; the shopping by rowing-boat across the bay; the dairy work and butter-making; as well as heavier outside work when the weather was good and the pressure was on. They were up baking before six in the morning, Janet producing a cairn of scones and Margaret one of pancakes. During the day, at the kitchen meals or the hayfield picnics, the scones and pancakes melted away, to be renewed in the endless dawn ritual which found the girls busy over the cooking range, with a great iron girdle apiece at the fire of mingled coals and peat.

A day or two after we started work at the Calve hay, Margaret had a birthday, and Seumas and I decided to mark the milestone by a baking of pancakes. That night, returned to the tent, I toiled late over the stove, dropping the batter with rapt zeal. I had always been proud of my pancakes. Baked in a tent by dim candlelight, and wolfed hot and hungrily direct from the pan, they had always been well received, and I had come to consider myself a cook of rich natural talents.

At the end of the rites for this special occasion we gathered up my output into newspapers, and the next day, the birthday morn, we produced it at the breakfast-table. But how different appeared the offering in the clear light of the day! How poor by comparison with the flawless mound of Margaret's own! Mine appeared to have suffered a congealing blight; they glistened with greasy rainbows, and fingerprints fouled them here and there; there were occasional soot plumes, or scorch marks from the pan; or sometimes their undersides were a shameless yellow dough, with only the faintest brushwork of brown to hint at the firing. Few of them were circular.

Our all too necessary words of deprecation were drowned in polite cries of 'Oh, but they're lovely!'—and the family stretched arms for them with eager courtesy, leaving Seumas and me to concentrate on Margaret's pancakes of that morning. As always, they were of velvet; light, symmetrical, homogeneous; utterly and rapturously perfect. A similar perfection baited Janet's scones, and we knew fearful indecision at meal-times, pausing in a momentary pleasant agony to make our minds up whether to start on the scones or the pancakes. Because one usually remained loyal to the first choice during an entire meal-time, so difficult was it to abandon one known perfection for another. It generally happened that Seumas and I would choose differently, and 'try the scones!' or 'try the pancakes!' we would counsel, full-mouthed, posting busily through our own selection.

The picture is not one of rough but wholesome fare, spiced by hunger born of open-air toil. It was a rich varied dietary, drawn largely from the land itself. Biscuits and fruit were almost the only food items bought in. Calum, like any good farmer, was a skilled butcher. He killed a lamb one day, and there followed a sequence of delights, spread over the meals of many days. First there was the blood. One of the girls came with a basin to collect, and we ate puddings at the next meal. The first breakfast after that was fried liver and kidneys; the first dinner, sheep's-head broth and boiled mutton. Roast leg of lamb came after, hot first and then cold, sliced for the hayfield sandwiches. Grilled chops made another breakfast or two. And so it went in a skilled succession, with the lamb's skin curing on a board to be a rug for the girls' bedroom.

These days, all of them, had a succulence in the air, drawn from the deep quality in the food which comes out of the Scottish soil. It is a real thing, not a memory glamoured to us personally now that a few years have passed. Not enough of our people here and elsewhere know about it, or how could we be persuaded that these pale and tasteless chunks of frozen meat, which are nowadays the main offerings of our diet, have even the same name, far less the same quality. This lamb had a mobile taste. It ran round the back of the teeth like an active spirit. When a fragment pressed the palate, there was an immediate and pervasive shock of taste, a gustatory delight, which spread and bloomed through all the senses.

These raptures made each meal-time an oasis in the long day. During the first period of our stay we were on Calve for about two weeks, working all that time on the hay crop, which had to be snatched at as the weather allowed. In some of the sunny days of high winds the hay made in the course of hours, and could be stacked before nightfall. There were other whole days when rain and spray flogged the island and laid the crop flat, so that it stood up painfully only after some warmth had taken off the burden of water. This hay, holding in its dry strips the refreshment of herds, went all winter to the cattle and the horses after the growing herbage was dead; and in its turn their mountainous dung was wheeled from the byre and stable to midden, thence to be scattered about the land and complete the clean and mysterious cycle of the harvest from which we all live.

A small strip of oats—called corn in Scotland—grew for late autumn harvesting, much of it to be milled for the meal, and the rest to sweeten, in whole sheaves, the feed of the animals. We helped to cut it in the back end, when we came back to Calve after our canoe trip was done. In the last week of October Calum was still fighting to take home his corn, and yet dealing softly with the raw young horse. He had a mechanical reaping machine to cut the stalks. All the rest—the gathering up, the binding and stooking—was the work of our hands.

There were also acres of potatoes and turnips. The turnips were the main root crop of the cattle feed, and Calum was able to grow them well on a peat-field which he had ploughed up for the first time in the previous year. He had planted the turnips experimentally in the peat, not expecting much, but hoping to get results sufficient to warrant a long move to bring this abandoned piece of land back among his arable fields. It was a successful essay. The year had been a dry and parched one, bad for turnips, which need great moisture. His own lay and swelled in the moist peat, and grew to be the best crop in the district. It was a triumphant tiny demonstration, for peaty land is looked on as land poisoned. By a fitting coincidence, it was on the fields of Mull, not far from Calve, where some of the first Highland experiments in turnip-growing were ever made.

The planting and delving of potatoes are probably the hardest of all farm tasks. We dug potatoes for whole days in early November, working for most of the daylight. Our red frozen hands clawed among the heavy earth, hooking up the potatoes into baskets which we dragged along the drills until they were caked with clay like great pots. To straighten up from this, and look over the bay towards Tobermory, was to rend the knotted sinews in the small of the back with a positive squeak. It was curious that this crouching pain grew less as the days passed, and in any case it could be stretched out of the system entirely five minutes after the last tattie had been lifted for the day.

There was, one evening, a strange flashing moment of contrast. We were carting in the bags of potatoes to the barn at the end of a day of brilliant autumn frost, when Calum lifted his head with a sudden comic gesture, hand on cheek, to a row of imaginary tenement windows, and moaned after the manner of coal hawkers. In that setting, that brilliance, it was a caricature to stun.

The tattie-howking is, however, at the time, a dour task, although it is the last of the island farm year. With the bagging and bringing in of the potatoes the major harvesting and stock labours are over. The winter gathers in around the steadings and the house. There is spare time to read and talk; time for the ceilidhs and the dances, and for winter holiday trips to Glasgow and Edinburgh. So it is with all Highland farms, and especially at Calve, set rarely apart in the sea, and peopled, as we knew it then, by the salt of the earth.

They were all perfectly bilingual, and we insisted on dispensing largely with English. Soon we struggled to a fair Gaelic fluency, hilariously tutored by any or all of the family. It was common for all work to be suspended as a linguistic point was made and developed, and a few more words added to our meagre vocabulary. Songs were sung by the dozen. There were classic stories to be heard by such experts as Locheil. The elderly character who was known by his chief's name was, of course, a Cameron who had settled at Tobermory for most of his lifetime, and as Mull is out of the Cameron territory, there was no reason why he should not have won and retained with dignity the nickname of Locheil. It was not a joke which would have been made in Lochaber. John Cameron was a man his clan might well be proud of. A great Gaelic story-teller, he had been a strong man and athlete in his youth, and until late in life he would accept any kind of hearsay challenge, but with good humour, to a feat of strength. We spoke to those who had seen him carrying a load of eight hundredweights of fencing wire. Somebody had told him (and it was probably untrue) that the strong man of a neighbouring parish had been seen carrying four two-hundredweight bales of wire at once, and youths were at hand to load a similar burden on Locheil. They let him seize one bale in each hand, and slung another two around his neck. Thus hung, he set off walking tremulously across a field, until, reaching a softer patch of soil, he was driven into the ground like a paling stob, with the grass level above his knees.

On another occasion the tale was brought to him of a rival muscle man who had proved himself so strong that he could sit himself in an oak wash-tub and lift the whole affair—self and tub— off the ground by the handles. I believe that Locheil got into a tub and wrenched upwards at the handles for an hour or two, endeavouring to lift the tubful of himself into the air. I believe also that he did this, not out of a muscular simplicity, but because he had the countryman's social sense which demands that a ploy of amusement or instruction is worth carrying out for the communal benefit, whether one is the butt or not.

Locheil had no enemies, and his friends were all who knew him. An old man and stiff in the joints, he spent the wet days before Hallowe'en dragging through the sodden leaves in the hazel woods gathering nuts, so that he might have them to give away in handfuls to the hosts of children who would come guising without shyness to his door.

A frequent visitor to the farm, he no sooner saw the canoes than he had to try one. We stuffed him in, his mighty spread of shoulders squared above the hull like a galley's mainsail, and pushed him off into the Sound. There he heaved himself up and down the sea-way, scooping gouts of water to the sky with the paddle blades, and making a great adventure of the affair. At last he came in to ground, bellowing a nautical judgment: "Hach, I could cross the Minch in her myself, and nothing in my hand but a spade!"

Locheil's talk and story kept the hayfield lively. In mid-morning, and again in mid-afternoon, the girls would come out from the farm-house with a great can of tea, a basket of cups and another of sandwiches. We would stick our forks and rakes in the ground and gather round the picnic. Anyone who has lost an appetite might well try a day at the hay. And later, he will not remember the work too well, but he will remember the tea-times. There was always a can of drammach standing by under the shade of a haycock. This drink is created by throwing two handfuls of oatmeal into a can of spring water. The cold cloudy liquid is an ancient thirst-quencher, and the oatmeal enthusiast can persuade himself to detect in it also a sustaining quality which is doubtless absent in a synthetic fruit drink.

It was a farm whose lines of communication were kept open by boats. The family were all rowers. The girls used to win the ladies' pairs at Tobermory Regatta with embarrassing ease, and it was a sight to see one of them, unflurried, and smartly dressed for town, skelping a heavy rowing-boat a mile or so across the bay to do the shopping and leave some milk. Every night there was the ritual of 'drawing the boats', when Calum and the sisters heaved the two or three rowing-boats, which were kept in commission at the tiny shore and jetty, up on to the shore turf above the highest spring tide-mark. This was a more dramatic performance during our second stay, when it was always done in a stormy pitch-darkness, with a hurricane-lamp standing on the rocks and throwing our immense Fingalian shadows on the barn gable. Hawsers ringed to iron bolts were lashed under the thwarts, and we would deploy indoors, with no link bridging the dark between us and the town.

The rattle of winter gave a special savour to our snug seclusion. This was the time for the kitchen dances, and we had one every second or third night. The MacKinnons would come from their house in the Aros woods, and other visitors would row out of the darkness, or would send piercing shepherd's whistles from the landing-stage across the Sound, until we rowed over and collected them. A horn gramophone was the music, and most of the guests could turn their hands to the 'box', or melodeon. Once we had a great celebration, almost a ball, in the stone-flagged kitchen, with a full orchestra of two melodeons and a fiddle. Reed and gut lift the heart-strings and the legs, and make the most persuasive of dancing accompaniments.

'I took pictures of the scenes by crude flashlight. The apparatus was the old-fashioned magnesium powder and touch-paper, which I had bought at a job price a day or two before leaving Glasgow. Both had grown damp in our travels, and required nursing to flash-point. The kitchen was lit by an oil-lamp, adequate for dancing, but dim for poring over smouldering explosive. The flashes, when they came, were of a devilish intensity, and left the kitchen in gross darkness, with the folk groping until their narrowed pupils picked up the lamp rays again. All this proved a merry interlude, and I was once even able to flee from the rusty tin lid on which the bomb was heaped, and get into the picture myself, before the apocalyptic chaos of the flare.

The dances were all quadrilles and other square or set figures. They were performed with accurate violence. A well-marked sense of rhythm is native to the Highlands, and the dancing is done with triumphant zest. There is none of the slipshod langour of the ballroom. In these parts the people who dance, dance well.

We also went in a house-party to the frequent dances in the Aros Hall in Tobermory, where the verve was as marked as in our kitchen reels. One finds the atmosphere of these village-hall affairs difficult to convey to the town dweller, without appearing to suggest a quaint scene of rustic clod-hopping. Actually, the proceedings were characterised by a gay and natural punctilio and correctness which is never seen in such town gatherings at all. There were none of the horseplay and antics which mark the ballroom's occasional ventures in Scottish dancing. In Mull the dances were known and enjoyed. It was a friendly affair; a native art, and living. And the music! In addition to the well-known dance airs, the musicians (led by the town butcher) had a limitless repertoire improvised from Gaelic songs, and one saw the unusual spectacle of a hall full of young people waltzing and singing at the same time, and doing both well.

City folk may well cut inept figures among such devotees. Ballroom dances are included to accommodate the hotel residents and other strangers who may make an appearance, but these items are flat-footed and lifeless by comparison with the rest of the programme. Other awkwardness may arise through a lack of wit. It has been mentioned that a certain decorousness underlies the merriment, and the point may well be missed by the urban stranger. The master of ceremonies at these dances has a wide authority for discipline which rarely requires to be exercised, but which can intervene at short notice, fortified, if necessary, by the support of all the other males in the hall. To the fellow of merry goodwill no harm will come. The mere rowdy will be asked to leave, and quickly.

Earlier in our summer a Royal Navy vessel had visited Tobermory, and the town arranged the courtesy of a dance for her crew. An unwise sailor, dancing with one of the girls, changed his protecting arm to a more amorous position. Shyly, the girl extricated herself, and then continued dancing normally with him. She was a slim and beautiful girl, and the fellow's crudity may have been the only tribute he knew how to pay. In a moment he was swash-buckling again, with increased pressure. Overwhelmed by embarrassment, his partner begged him to release her, and got for a reply a knowing towny laugh and a further advance. It was a situation undreamt of among her own kind; but an adolescence devoted to work on the land and in rowing-boats had fitted her for what was probably the only method of dealing with the situation.

She stepped back from his grasp, measured him momentarily with her left hand, and struck him in the face with her right. It was a dread blow, and it felled him. It did not merely fell him to the ground. The sailor had rashly chosen, as the site of his advances, the top of the open stairway which led from the dance floor to the entrance hall below. He went down this flight in a half-conscious bundle, and on the top of him fell, by intent, a handful of Tobermory lads who had seen the incident and were on their way for him anyway. By a quirk of civilised restraint, they grasped him with firmness, but did him little harm. Instead, he was taken somewhere and revived. It is one of his shore adventures he will never be heard to boast of.

During all the separate days of our Calve stay, when the north trip was still to do, we were alert to our chances for pushing on. We also did a great deal of canoe handling, enough to smooth off some of the unskilled edges, and were much afloat in the heavy conditions which pinned us there, keeping us back from the open waters. There was one day when, during the whole morning, an easterly gale which had come up with the sun turned the whole bay white, and filled the Sound past the farmhouse windows with an endless rending curtain of spray. Something urgent was wanted in the way of mails from the post office, but the morning went on and still there was no chance of putting off one of the boats. We were claiming all the time that the canoes could travel on this over to Tobermory; the gale would be well aft of our beam, and would take us fast. It was the kind of short stiff test we were eager for. Eventually we pushed the canoes off and, paddling hard, went away down the Sound like shavings down a river.

We never experienced so much motion before nor since. Most of the water was surf, and the canoes twisted all the way through a mad ellipse, with never more than half the keel-length in the water. We were too busy to watch the town, but we must have been a sight for those who came down to the end of the old pier to see us come through the spray, with our bows skying and digging. It was a bracing few minutes, set into another perspective by the banker's wife, who pressed forward to say as we landed: 'Are you two married? . . . Because if you are I'm sorry for your wives!'

On many other occasions, this was a familiar type of greeting for us. At all points, sympathy was lavished on our wives, whom we had not yet encountered. Seumas quotes, as the most notable case of transferred sympathy on record, one which occurred farther north. It had been a brutal end to the day, with a twilight bump ashore on a bad beach and a sodden painful scramble over rocks. He trotted over to a distant cottage and knocked on the door. A woman opened. She stared at him; his dripping and inadequate clothes, his battered shin-bones, his salty face; and exclaimed (they were her first words): 'Oh, your poor mother!'

Tobermory, however, was by no means entirely negative, for even a certain proprietary concern had made the town interested in us. One of the merchants strolled to his door that wild day to tell us as we passed on the pavement: 'I was just saying to a lady in the shop "It's a fierce day indeed. You won't see the Canoe Boys out to-day"—and then, by Jove, there you were!'

Hallowe'en came on us when we were again at Calve at the end of October. This was a full-scale festival, with clear-cut divisions for the children and for the grown-ups. Tobermory went gaily *en fête*, although, as we remember, the night of the 31st of October was wet and bitter cold. First came the sallies of the children, scampering in fancy dress from house to house; singing their songs from behind false-faces for rewards of nuts and apples; or steaming the windows of family homes with the uproar of parties, and dooking for apples. Later they were bundled off to bed, and the younger grown-ups took up the play.

The Calve contribution to the festival had been in preparation for some days. Some welcome time had been taken off from the potato-gathering to row across to the Aros shore and gather the nuts as they dropped thickly from the hazel-trees above the tide-mark. There had also been gleeful discussions about costumes, with the girls planning surprises for friends into whose homes they would thrust Seumas and me, without ceremony. For it is part of the ancient Hallowe'en rite and jest that you may enter any house, disguised as you will, and sit with the folk talking or silent, while they try to guess who you are. We were rehearsed in the domestic trivia of some of the homes which were likely to be victims of these incursions. A set of ghastly cardboard false-faces was laid in stock. But on the night of Hallowe'en, as we were preparing, Janet refused to wear one of these impassive disguises. She stretched instead a fine hand up the kitchen chimney, took off a handful of soot, and rubbed this becomingly into her face.

Seumas was our prize exhibit. He went forth with us to the shore as an elderly and leering dowager, in a costume of black silk skirt and a leg-of-mutton-sleeved black silk blouse with sequins. This was produced from a kist by Mrs. MacDonald, and it fitted Seumas very well here and there, even about the waist, which, in view of later developments in that area, is a feat worth remembering. He also wore it with style, and his pallid and eyeless mask was leprously repulsive. As an after-thought he carried with him a matronly bundle of knitting.

This was the figure which, plying an erratic pair of needles, was lurched into the door of the MacKinnons' house at Aros. The rest of us, having hidden behind the trees, clustered forward to the parlour window to watch him sit in the chimney-corner and embark on a searching series of enquiries in falsetto about their recent family history. They gathered round him, guessing in vain, the girls baffled not only by the lithe figure, but by his knitting technique, as he stabbed two-handed among the un-purling rows of stitches. At last we laughed our way through the door and gave him away.

We got 'fuarag' in this house. It is the equivalent of the Lowland 'champit tatties', the Hallowe'en dish in which the participants dip among the mashed potatoes with spoons, eating the mash and searching for favours. The Gaelic 'fuarag' is a much superior dish. It consists of a large bowl of slightly soured whipped cream, into which is stirred a quantity of oatmeal grains which have been toasted in the oven. The favours are tossed among this, and dipped for in the darkness, the party supping tensely, and biting from time to time on the bachelors' buttons, old maids' thimbles, dolls, bells, rings, and sixpences. The dish was lavishly riddled with these items. We all got one or more, and many a spoonful of delight as well.

Later we went into Tobermory and practised our deceits upon the citizens there. Seumas and I now had good enough Gaelic to answer the more simple inquisitions, but were always discovered at last, amid shouts of: 'The Canoe Boys!' Our costumes were all less distinctive than Seumas's, but more concealing. Janet's handsome negress deceived no one, and readily identified our party, but the individual labels were hard to fix. The innkeeper of the Mishnish Hotel tumbled on a ruse to force us to remove the false-faces. He brought us great glasses of sherry on a salver. But we poured the stuff crudely between the wilting lips of our masks, and got only some of it internally. There was a piper or two, and we and the other guerrilla bands of guisers danced on the piers and about the whole main street, the elders at the upper windows helping the illuminations by shedding torchlight on us. So we wore much of the night away before rowing back over the familiar water.

Since this time, Calve has been sold, and as I write these lines it is for sale again. For Seumas and me, we must always feel about the island as we shall about any land where people have been happy, and we with them. It had been for us a symbol of what we had come to find: a proof that we had a goal at all. In token of which it gave us a share of itself for ever, and took as much in return. Whoever buys Calve can never wholly own it. Whoever sells it off may not displenish our memories.

CHAPTER XI

ARDMORE

> They challenged him: 'Leave folly's toil behind—
> Your fortune's furth and further!' Comes the day
> He scrapes upon the nettled land to find
> The treasure that this wisdom threw away.

IT was time to be going. The south-westers still blew in a long sequence of three-day tumults, with pauses between of sometimes only a few hours, and it was well into September.

Our next stage would be the most dangerous open-water passage of the trip—round Ardnamurchan, the farthest west point of the British mainland; a buttress of rock hammered endlessly by the Atlantic, and without a shore for miles. The account of this hazard makes disturbing reading in all the navigational journals, and even the most optimistic of our Tobermory friends could not desist from a repeated warning: 'It's too late in the year for Ardnamurchan!'

From the high ground of Calve we could look over to the ready-made weather-gauge which betrays the sea conditions at the Point itself. This was the group of the Stirk Rocks. They lie two miles off at Auliston Point at the end of Loch Sunart in Morven. 'If the sea is breaking on the Stirks, it's bad outside', is the Mull wisdom. There was one whole day when, on all our high dashes to view them at their sea-pastures, we saw no sign of them shaking the swell off their flanks. On the next morning they seemed to be still docile. The seas from outside, sent by a wind which was still hearty from the southward, rolled at them, but there was no broken spouting.

So there started at last the old frenzy of packing, with the tent coming down and the rounding up of our gear, so much more dispersed than if we had arrived the night before. The grass of our camp site was pale and flattened. A few days longer, and we might have wintered in that hollow, like tinkers. It was past midday before the last bundle was tamed to its travelling shape

12. THE DESERTED FARM AT ARDMORE
Seumas sits to the right of our fire, which blazes in the black space where the grate has been. I have just scrambled into the picture, having fired our damp flash powder after several vain attempts.

13. THE CEILIDH BAND AT CALVE. *Malcolm MacDonald, the farmer, is on the right. The dark halo behind his head is the horn of the gramophone, the alternative source of music for our dances, which we held every second or third night.*

14. THE AUTHOR AT ARDMORE. *Fourteen years later I am standing on the spot where I am seen sitting in picture 12 overleaf. The whole roof has fallen in and the floorboards have rotted away. But is this the end of Ardmore?*

and stuffed out of sight, and the canoes were riding the Sound water, anchored only by their points resting on the shingle.

We had a quick stand-up kitchen meal, and got off at last, hailed away by all the household and the dogs. The girls went up to an attic window to wave us out of sight, while the rest went back to the long fight with the hay.

There was no hurry. We meant to get within striking distance of Ardnamurchan Point by the middle afternoon, at slack water, and take the making tide northwards. We could do this without pressing, and were glad enough at the prospect. Although the recent small trips in the bay, and the deliberate practice, had refined our paddling style and brought a noticeable new flair, these were laden canoes, and had a drag on them.

We skirted the little coast of Calve outwards to the open water, feeling again splendidly self-contained, by way of compensation for the loss of the homestead warmth. The town of Tobermory fell away on our left, its last outpost, beyond the gables of the most seaward houses, being the great white-painted phrase on the cliff above the swimming-boxes: 'God is Love'. This announcement has been there for fifty years, a strange reminder that even the most austere Calvinism needs its wayside shrines.

Soon the heavier wind of the Sound of Mull was in our hair— and there was the lighthouse of Rudha nan Gall! We brushed its very skirts, getting a wave from the balcony. Here with the Sound widening away towards the sea we recognised again the familiar sensation we had forgotten for a little time—the receding of land, and the readjustment of the mind to the different moving solidity of the sea. But we were still shore fowl, for it was possible to use Mull as a screen for some miles yet, and this we did as we held in to the little cliffs of the Mishnish shore on our left.

There was a good deal of history about us. Soon we were crossing the mouth of Bloody Bay, scene of a scrambling fifteenth-century sea-fight by claimants for the Lordship of the Isles, whose sea skill was of course prodigious, but was rarely exercised in set-piece naval battles. Away over on the Ardnamurchan shore opposite, like a hollow tooth, was the shell of Mingary Castle. It saw more than its share of the same war, changing hands many times, and in the end a Scottish monarch sat in court there to receive the submission of all the Isles pretenders.

From Ardnamurchan Point we would go north with the tide, round the headland and out to the little island of Muck, or some other of the Small Isles group. There came a rising wind from the south again, and although this was the right direction, its strength was something more than comfortable. So, reaching the scattered rocks of Ardmore Point, at the far side of Bloody Bay, we lay there afloat for half an hour, at the most northerly point of Mull, anchored by long strands of exposed seaweed which we squeezed under the cockpit flaps to hold us. Here we had shelter from the wind, and as it was off-shore, there was only a little sea where we sat.

At the back of four o'clock, the bottom of the tide, we tore out our rubbery anchor cables and paddled off round Ardmore Point, heading for Ardnamurchan. At once a blast of wind skidded us sideways and outwards towards the cliffs north of the Sound, where we could see, even from our low viewpoint, the white fringe of spray rising. Ardmore shore, hardly half a mile away on our left, was lost in the wicked whipped sea-gale which poured like a waterfall over the shore hills, and, cold and solid, drove us out to sea. It carried us, more skidding than pointing; and this was no way to face Ardnamurchan, and these were not the conditions.

So we turned shorewards, seeking the shelter of the fresh and green weathered slopes, where the wind, pounding downwards like water falling, was combing the bracken and the grass. We were better canoeists than we had been the last time the canoes were laden, but this was no paddle across Tobermory Bay, and we set to the bitterest struggle of all our journey. We do not know now how long it took us to cover these few hundred yards, but the evening seemed to grow dark while we laboured. For long spells at a time we made no headway at all, the poles of our paddles bending as the blades tore the water apart, and we leaned far forward to dodge the wind. Then we would be making headway a little, in inches only, and grunting down the gale. The windows of a house which stood on a snug shelf, backing to the sea, stared at us impassively, but no one came out to watch.

There was one moment when we knew we would get in, although much heaving was still ahead. When we touched the steep shore at last, and got out, we lay on the cold stones with our legs shaking. But this was soon over; the twangling sinews of our arms felt fine, and restored again. Seumas went scrambling over the hill towards the house, to report ourselves and save the inhabitants the hour or two of scouting to which they would otherwise have to resort on the appearance of tented strangers from the sea. I heaved the canoes up above the high-water mark. In such a casual description it sounds a little feat. The shore was steeply sloping and composed of stones as loosely packed as a rough-riding paddock, so that my bare legs sank to mid-calf. Each canoe, packed with gear and aswill with water, weighed no less than a hundred and fifty pounds; and I rushed them successively up to the grass without a pause. I shall remember this breenge with zest in later and stiffer times. Then I unpacked the stuff, assembled it for portaging, and de-watered and snugged down the canoes in the browning bracken.

Seumas came loping down the hill slope, shouting first, and when nearer telling that the house was empty and in the first stages of ruin. No one was living in the glen of Ardmore. We shouldered our bundles and climbed inland to the house. It backed on to the last knoll before the edge of the hill, so that only its roof could be seen from the Sound of Mull. In front, it faced a sweet level of the greenest turf, which was being strangled by bracken not many yards from the door. Around, and disappearing in the undergrowth and thickets, were other and more ancient ruins.

We took possession of the house. It was a room-kitchen-and-scullery place on the ground floor, with wooden stairs leading from the small lobby to the loft attics overhead. The door hung ajar on one hinge. There was no glass in the windows. While the kitchen half was intact, the slates had started to slide from the roof of the ben end. In the kitchen, the space from which the grate had been torn had left a hole gaping like the mouth of a cave. We gathered armfuls of dry heather and old wood from the outhouses, and got a monstrous fire going, so that steam arose from the damp furred floorboards. Our cheerful smoke, with a plume of sparks, flew bravely from the chimney.

The smoke, as it bloomed, already helped to people the valley. Standing on the knoll behind, we lingered to admire our housekeeping. The solid back of the little building, unlike the weathered front, gave no sign of decay. It might have been a live homestead, warm with folk. And very comfortable they could have been there.

Turning round to face the sea, a more formidable sight lay over from us. In the darkening grey the point of Ardnamurchan was immense, with its miles-long base in the heaving sea fringed with the darting points of white where surf was climbing the rocks. We could almost, over the wide stretch of the Sound, hear the roar of it, and the hiss as it spread back some cables' length from the ramparts. There was, however, enough noise where we were, for the gale was in spate down Ardmore valley like a burn of wind, and we went back to the warm kitchen, barricaded the door, hung the sails, loaded with stones, as panes of canvas instead of glass in the windows, and perched lit candle-ends here and there to wag and lowe in the draughts. Something better than this kind of weather would be necessary before we could take the northern course round Ardnamurchan.

But, in journeys like these, each stage can be planned for only adequately, and taken then as the time seems best. Once the course is studied and decided, there is no gain in wrestling to carry the mind beyond the body. So once more we sloughed away our little worries and lay on our backs upon groundsheet-covered bracken beds, basking in the heartening fire. The dark fell down the valley, and we had to go outside several times in delight to see the hot chimney breathing redly upon the under-side of our smoke. We cooked a lengthy supper in the fire-hole, scraping a bowl or two of milkless brose; and then washing down pavements of bread and cheese with black gallons of milk-less tea. We had a musical session, on a timid tin whistle and a mouth-organ. And, sitting late at the ingle, we talked back and forward about ourselves. Before bedtime, I rigged up the camera and the dampening heap of flash powder, opened the lens shutter, lit a reluctant flare, and scrambled back to my place in the chimney-corner before the flare wuffed off, heaving up the roof slates with a tiny rattle. Then we dowsed the candles; and, lying in our quilt bags, we watched the fire embers die as sleep came on us.

The next morning showed no change in the weather, and we could not go on. We spent the morning in a survey of our demesne, and the pattern of its old and rich life which we were able to piece from the broken fragments that lay about. These were later filled in, when we sought such old records as are available, as well as from the people now alive in the north-west of Mull, who can remember, by the true hearsay of their youth, what had been done here.

Ardmore had been a hamlet of strong men and their families. Their unroofed cornerless houses pushed walls up here and there above the tide of bracken, like wrecks reluctant at the end to lay their timbers on the sea-bed. There had been, at the time of the place's most recent heyday, about ten of these houses. They had stood on the first step of the low hills above the valley floor. What had been a village green of perfect turf still lived in a few reefs of its pure herbage over which the bracken had not yet crawled.

If I am told, as one tends to hear in such cases, that these people were able to scrape only a wretched living from the ground, and were better dispersed on their emigrant business, I shall require proof more persuasive than is usually available. And I shall be able to maintain, I think, that none of their scattered descendants now enjoys a view like the one left behind on the broken Ardmore doorsteps.

Each of these homes possessed at least eight cattle, and other beasts upon the hill. They would have ample milk and butter and cheese, and red meat, and poultry, and their own oatmeal and potatoes and other crops. They had the fruit berries that are still there thickly, and the game. They had the choice of fish too; shell-fish for the lifting, to be stewed in milk; lobsters to trap and herring to net. But they were also connoisseurs of the delicate varieties of sea-food. They used to catch close inshore the sea-bream and the gurnet, scattering shells into the water to stir the fish upwards towards the nets. These sorts of fish are the ones which have been dispersed by the illegal mechanical trawling of inshore waters.

All this, and doubtless much else on a far from niggardly scale, must have given a hearty fullness to the old Ardmore days. There was a school with thirty pupils; and on the shore and the glen slopes near by there was plenty of adventure for the scholars when they skailed. The little village was four miles from Tobermory, and the track is still good that leads from the Glengorm road round the mild slopes of the Mishnish hills, to spread and lose itself at last on what was the Ardmore village green, ringed now by these empty ruins. There are those still alive who knew people reared in Ardmore when it was like this. And I dare say, if you were to start telephoning round all these Mac-Leans we have been talking about, who would answer the call in Chicago or Toronto or London, you would sooner or later be speaking to one whose grandfather ran barefoot and well fed upon Ardmore Point.

That was, then, the original phase of life at Ardmore. Its trails are clear, and it lasted for at least a handful of centuries. The second phase was shorter. It is represented by the house in which we had installed ourselves—the farm built to handle the whole glen, once rid of its people. It had also failed, as we know, and that in a time shorter than an eyeblink of history. The solitary house, and the system of husbandry and lairdship,it signified, had not even a hint of the endurance of the community that had been there; and that might, if management and understanding had been nearer home, have been there yet. The house itself may last a shorter time than the old blockhouse shapes of the village. A year or two after the war I walked over to it from Tobermory in a little over an hour. The whole roof has now come in, and such rafters as still hang by their ends to the ceiling level of the walls are rotten, and shedding off their slates like leaves on to the floor which is now earth, for the planking has gone. Around the ruin were huddled the stupid victors of the third phase of Ardmore, as we saw them on that first day of our residence—the sheep. Because the glen, like so many of the others, has come to a sheep run at the last; and it will hardly, on the souring ground, carry as many sheep as it did people. But there may be a fourth phase to come—the fourth segment of the circle.

By mid-afternoon we knew we could not set off that day to round the Point. We did not care to walk in to Tobermory and the shops, although we needed to, for our food was low and our eating tremendous. For the midday meal I had baked bread. This pretentious description was applied by me to a revolting device which consisted of dampening several handfuls of flour with water, dropping the tacky mixture into a tin, setting this by the fire, and drying out the moisture again. The result was a fat and warm wafer which it was expedient to eat fresh from the tin, and in the mirk of the kitchen. We had travelled light from

Calve, and all that now remained were the little basic sacks of oatmeal, flour, and dried fruit.

Replenishments were, however, at hand. Rabbits ran in droves about the lawns, sallying from one to another of the bracken clumps in that strangely jerked creeping run which, perhaps more than any other quality, entitles them to the description of vermin. We started to hunt them, running and whooping among the green clearings, with stones for ammunition. We filled the air with missiles, and were contemptuously treated by our victims. The rabbits appeared to be able to hobble slowly from the path of even our deadliest shots, and much energy was spent before we abandoned the undisciplined hunt, to lay tactics for a more certain manœuvre.

Made cunning by hunger, we stalked a long way inland through the bracken, and then started a gentle drive back towards the open grass. By this time we knew the most prominent holes, and were able to steer a tiny herd past them all and out of the bracken. Here at last we cornered a small plump fellow, penning him in a sheep-fank. I herded him gradually up into a cul-de-sac, while Seumas, with an adequate stone, ran along the top of the dyke to reach a mortar position above the prize.

Tense at my post, I saw the stone rise in Seumas's hand, and felt a pang of grief for our dinner, still warm on the paw, but doomed. Then Seumas tossed the stone aside and clapped his two hands to scare the rabbit into scrambling free; and then turned to grin ruefully at me: 'Couldn't do it!' he said, with none of the ruthlessness of the hunter. Awaiting the death-blow, the rabbit had crouched low and panting on the green, putting his ears flat back and rolling his shrinking eyes upward. This had been too piteous a sight for Seumas. With appetites grossly worked up by our exertions, we went back intrepidly to the fireplace, and cooked and ate another hideous disc of dough.

In the night the wind slackened. The morning brought a struggling sun and a light which showed the seas breaking more gently on Ardnamurchan. So it was back to the packing again, the long scramble up and down to the shore, the stowing and trimming and stripping for the fray afloat. We could not launch, because of the tide, until well into afternoon. But there we were at last, away from Mull, with Ardmore Bay receding, and the open seas coming up hard on the wind to our left as we lost the land.

All along, Ardnamurchan Point had been the pondered obstacle. Most of our hazards so far had come on us quickly, but this was one we knew of, and there was a release of elation to be now spearing the Point with our bows. It was a gradual building-up of effect as we went on this leg north, with greater and greater seas gathering up under us, and the wind behind them. We were frail enough, but we were the first objects the waves had met since mid-Atlantic.

By the time the canoes were half-way between Mull and the Point we were amongst an enormous motion. This was the full Atlantic swell, more than a hundred yards from crest to crest. In the valleys we lost all sight of the land, and even felt no wind until we lifted again almost to the top of the weather slope of the new wave. We paddled many yards apart, and were out of sight of each other for seven seconds or more at a time. It was a sight to remember for a lifetime, as Seumas slid up the wave slope away from me, hung high on the crest with his keel showing, and the green daylight through the water under him. Then he would seem to fall over the far edge, and vanish. But I would rise in my turn, alone and unseen, and eventually poise on a ridge; and there he would be in the next valley, paddling surely, and we would be together again for seconds more. The surfaces of these great waves were pitted with smaller waves borne along with them, some of them breaking. We were able to meet each breaker as it came, although it was a new problem to have to encounter these, as it were, on the side of a hill, and not on an even keel.

At times, when it was possible to do more than glance, I would see Seumas yawning widely. This was an involuntary gant to which he was subject in broken water. It seemed to be brought on by the saturation of his throat with the briny air. It was, under the lively conditions, in no way a signal of boredom or indifference! Hereabouts, Seumas lost a bandage which had been hampering him. Two days before, as we were making ourselves comfortable at Ardmore, a branch of firewood had slashed him across the thumb, cutting almost to the bone. He still has the scar, but it speaks much for our fitness that the wound was already closed, and the salt water washed the bandage off and away.

As we went farther there was more wind, and occasionally,

not far from us, one of the main waves would itself break and explode like a depth charge and send along a heaving crest of white, travelling fast, and as great as a villa roof. We lost a little time through being wary of these breakers, paddling quickly off the crests if they seemed restless, or shouldering up to them if retreat was too late. We had fortune in that we never had one breaking where we sat, but the vigilance kept us occupied, and when we were well enough accustomed to this sailing to look around casually, it was to find ourselves well abreast of the face of Ardnamurchan. Three miles ahead, we could see for the first time the slim needle of the lighthouse which is Britain's first signal westward.

We kept at least a mile off the land as we went, for there was a great inshore commotion at the cliff-foot, and white water was climbing and booming on the rocks. A thick shadow of cloud suddenly darkened the day above us, and we turned to see a Fleetwood trawler coming up astern on the end of his smoke, as if he were fussing along on a tattered leash. They saw us, and came alongside, slowing down. The skipper came to his bridge window, pointing and beckoning, offering us a lift. He was near, but also had the binoculars on us, since in that water the dark blue canvas must have been hardly visible, and we would appear like two men walking waist-deep. But we waved him on. By this time all his crew were at the rail, and the whistle was blowing at us. They waved their way ahead. It was fearsome to see how they rolled, with their masts and funnel almost pushing under.

Abreast of Ardnamurchan Lighthouse we ate our sandwiches, myself handing his to Seumas on the blade of the paddle, and he snatching as we slid and climbed. From here the isle of Muck was due north, but it was lost in a sea-haze. We had never before gone round Ardnamurchan without seeing, not only the Small Isles, with near Muck, the unforgettable skylines of Eigg and Rhum, and distant Canna, but also the Cuillins of Skye. To-day there was a dark veil, and it was into this we stroked for the last eight miles.

Here was a very eerie experience. We took a course by the pocket-compass on the island ahead which we could not see, and set off firmly, for the day was passing. Behind us, Ardnamurchan grew fainter and was taken into the mist, while ahead, no land broke the veil. It was a strange and unsought moment of navigation, and the sea seemed great and dark, with all its ceaseless immediate problems, and this wider one as well. But as we pressed on, the hills of Rhum, high up, came first, and then, in front, the near low ground of the Muck shore.

Two hours of strong paddling from the lighthouse brought us to some shelter eastward of the south point of Muck. The harbour of Port Mor faced us, dyked by skerries at its entrance. We were now tiring, and the dusk was coming; so instead of taking the proper channel through, between the patches of Dubh-Sgeir and Bogha Rudha, we sneaked in westward of Dubh-Sgeir, among surfing fangs of rock. After rounding Ardnamurchan Point, and coming this length, we were, we felt, entitled to fortune. In this precarious manner we passed safely into the harbour bay, and took easily the half-mile leg in to the little pier. All the way, there grew upon its short concrete top a lengthening row of spectators. Before we came alongside they numbered about twenty—at least two-thirds of the total population. Among the first words we heard as we stepped out and lifted up the canoes were: 'You'll be hungry. Come in and have your tea!'

The houses of the village made a little row along the shore of the inner harbour. We pitched our tent at the head of the bay, and soon were eating and thawing at a spread table before a kitchen fire. It was dark before the eating and the talk were over. One of the sons improvised a lantern from a candle stuck into a glass jam-jar, and lit us round to the tent. Some of the men crouched inside with us for a while and talked more. And then they went away—and oh, the sleep! . . . the sleep!

We stayed for three days in Muck. It is the most southerly of the group of four inhabited Small Isles—Rhum, Eigg and Canna are the others. The Gaelic etymology is obscure, and this makes tolerable the wit which, in an Anglicised setting, has given them the ingenious nickname of the Cocktail Isles. The Small Isles form a parish of Inverness-shire, Eigg being the headquarters of such common services as the minister, the Roman Catholic priest, and the doctor. These travel by motor-boat on their administrations from island to island, when the weather allows. The main transport headquarters is Muck, in whose ownership and anchorage is the strong motor-boat which services the inter-island needs. The isles, all but Muck, are precariously on the telephone. Muck is also excluded from the steamer calls which touch the other three twice a week or so. The whole group is a scattering of land lumps immediately to the south of Skye, and level with Barra, the most southerly of the Outer Hebrides. Eigg and Canna are the two most visited. Rhum is inhospitable by proprietorial intent, and Muck's bad coast and off-shore waters tend to keep even the cruising yachtsmen away.

Accordingly we were greatly welcomed, and the whole of the first forenoon was devoted to an inspection of the canoes. Before evening, almost every soul in the island—men, women, and children—had been embarked for a solo paddle in the bay. Most of the younger people, adept in boats, were at home instantly in the novel structure. The only grossly unskilled, but by no means uneasy, passenger was the island herdsman, a born landlubber, although no part of his range was above half a mile from the sea, and a considerable sea at that.

Muck is immensely fertile. The laird, Mr. MacEwan, farms almost the whole of it, apart from the small croft lands about the harbour. He showed us enthusiastically round the rich knolls and valleys of his land. At that time he was spending his winters ski-ing in Switzerland and the rest of the year farming in Muck—an entrancing blend. In his hayfields, the haystacks jostled one another, so thick had been the growth. His fat sheep ambled and gorged the ripe grass. On the west side of the island we saw an agricultural prodigy—fields and acres of carrots flourishing. The carrot-fly disease is unknown here, and the endless wind lifts an endless spray of the powdered-shell sand from the beach on to the fields, which enjoy a steady snow of lime.

The carrots were mighty, and great also was our enthusiasm to spread the news of this fertility. This led us to overreach ourselves in the matter of Press illustrations, for the story we got ready to send about Muck would be better, we judged, if one of the outsize carrots could accompany it. We obtained such a carrot from the laird and wedged it into the cardboard container from a whisky bottle, coiling its long delicate tail round the inside of the parcel. The whole was wrapped and tied, and addressed, along with the story, to the late celebrated John James Miller, at that time the agricultural editor of the *Daily Record*. We learned later that when the parcel arrived in his mail in its familiar shape, he tore it joyfully open. His rage was dreadful when he pulled forth, instead of a bottle, the earthy club of carrot which had been our proud exhibit, and he hurled it from him. It lodged in one of the immense waste-paper containers which buoy editorial floors, and the Muck carrots never got a mention.

One of the lads of the motor-boat took our story and the carrot parcel to post in Tobermory on their next trip. We waved the launch away, on a bright morning, and soon struck our tent and stowed gear for the journey to Eigg, the nearest island to the north. This time we went through the proper passage, and at once hit the swell, still heaving up from the south-west, and therefore going with us.

The whole island came to watch us on our way, and even the school came out. They lined the low brae on the eastern shore in a long waving row, and a little apart stood the laird, offering us his salute. It was an ancient sight, a picture of distinction, that we saw from the cockpits. The spectacle they saw was more mobile. We were out of sight oftener than in it, and we laughed, as we climbed and fell again, to see them straining to detect us among the water, and then pointing suddenly, and waving again, as we appeared.

It was a zestful time, probably for all. For us two, it relieved a preoccupation which had become pressing in the last week or two. None of the newspaper articles had yet been paid for, and it would still be some time before the monthly accounting would catch up.

It is probably the only drawback to a completely carefree exploration of one's own country that one may not live off the land, since the land is inhabited by fellow-citizens whose life is also on a sterling basis. This is as it should be, but at the time it made our case awkward. So far we had paid our way. Leaving Muck, we had bought eggs and scones, and persuaded the folk to take payment for some of the kindly hospitality they had given.

Here we were now, afloat, and our total cash amounted to four shillings and sevenpence.

CHAPTER XII

THE FORBIDDEN ISLAND

> Bring up your batteries,
>   This Twelfth is Glorious!
> (Mind, though, your flatteries—
>   'Sweet-song-and-story' us)
> Triumph of alien one—
>   Freedom is loot for you!
> Kings of this people run
>   Gillie-wet-foot for you.

EIGG rides the inner Minch like a ship. The island's unmistakable shape can be seen from mainland peaks far into the heart of Scotland. Five miles long, it lies as if travelling from south to north, with a trawler bow almost a thousand feet high, a dip down to a central well-deck, and a battlemented poop rising to thirteen hundred feet. This galleon shape is the central spine of the island, breaking in cliffs along the middle of the land, and shielding, at their feet, green fields and crofts. The 'poop' is the splendid peak, the Sgurr, and it was for the harbour at its base, in the south of the island, that we were making.

We had six miles of open water to cross, but once into the swing of the great swell we found the passage easy. We got a squall of rain half-way over which blotted out the island for many minutes, and chilled us more than the gouts of sea. As we came up to the red cliffs of the south shore, the caves there opened their mouths at us. The sea was hammering the reefs off Castle Island, sending white streaks out back into the channel. Where the channel narrows we rounded the point of the pier suddenly, seeing below us the yellow sand of the shallows.

We were very fresh, and it was no more than midday, when we came aground on the concrete slope of the pier. There was no one to be seen at the sheds, nor around any of the trim houses in sight. We bundled into some bushes, flinging off our bleached paddling clothes, and spreading them to the air. In a few moments we were kilted and shod, and on the road towards the centre of the island.

We had a dashing encounter with two small Eigg citizens, at an intersection of roads which puzzled us about our proper direction. A small girl of about six appeared, leading a tiny infant by the hand. It was an infant at that stage when, seen walking, they look even tinier than a babe in arms, and the pace it was setting was an almost imperceptible forward stacher. Here was an opportunity to have a neutral verdict on our Gaelic. We approached the pair gently, not to frighten them, and the following conversation went through in Gaelic without a hitch:

'Which is the road to the post office?'
'That's it yonder.'
'Great thanks to thyself, O little girl.'

We went forward in terrific gratification, glowing in the tribute paid by our little pathfinder, who, unlike her older relatives, could not have been tempted to help us out in English, as she had probably a very hazy knowledge of that language. We turned back to wave to her, and she waved without shyness, and also revolved the incredibly small child on its axis, so that he was looking eventually in our direction and could wave too. These two made a brave little picture on the down side of the brae from us, with sixty miles of the Scottish coast for their backcloth.

It was a post office and grocery store combined: indeed, a co-operative store, with the isles folk shareholders, and dividends going at the end of the year. I had the melancholy first task of wiring home for three pounds, by way of an advance against the newspaper fees we would eventually get. This was a delicate piece of telegram compilation, to find an economical and yet not too disturbing form of words.

Incoming mail awaited us in the form of letters and a packet or two. The packets had been forwarded through Mallaig post office, where Mrs. Watt the postmistress (we did not know her yet) had printed heavily across one of them: 'Canoe Boys! Weary waiting for you! Hurry up and give us a call! P.O. Mallaig.' It was a friendly shattering of the post office rules, and our hearts warmed to the knowledge that we had a following.

We also failed to buy any bread, as the steamer was not due

until the next day with a consignment of Glasgow-made loaves. But 'Mrs. MacDonald down at the shore will make you a baking of scones.' This news we announced to Mrs. MacDonald herself, who heard it bravely at the door of her beautiful cottage. She had a family of sons, and was accustomed to hungry emergencies. By the time we had the tent up and the tea going, the scones were ready, a biscuit tin full of treacle and soda scones, and she filled our bonnets with eggs too.

It wasn't hard to find business in Eigg which kept us five days there. Everybody had to paddle the canoes round the bay, and some of the folk came from the bigger settlement, at Cleadale on the west side, to get their turn. There was the Sgurr to climb, caves to explore, the minister, the priest, and the doctor to visit. The Muck boys came one day in their boat on ferry affairs, and they had to see the canoes again. There was also the hope that the wind, now round dead to the west, would die a little and let us get to Rhum. For it was essential that we take in Rhum on our way. We wrote some things, and mended our clothes; and as the thickets at our tent door abounded with the ripest brambles, we bought sugar in the store and made a great boiling of jam, which went onwards with us on the trip, in an aluminium pot which never thereafter got rid of the purple dye.

The church, the school, and the post office are strung out along the top of the ridge where the road, rising from the hamlet at the harbour, crosses the spine of the island to reach Cleadale on the far shore. Here they provide a centre for spiritual, mental and bodily services within energetic reach of all the homesteads of the island. The siting of these common buildings exposes them, of course, to heavy weather up there on the middle heights. The Roman Catholic church and the priest's house have a cosier setting among the croft houses of Cleadale, looking over to the Outer Isles.

But on the day we attended the parish church, the Sunday, it was in a brilliant atmosphere, with the sun polishing the scene out of all recognition by artists or photographers. The church has clear windows, and as we stood to sing the psalms our eyes stared round, and our breath caught, at the immense glory of the scene. For the church, on its height, forms as it were a pulpit on the Western Isles, and dominates them all. From window after window there are views to move the soul of man. On that

Sunday the sky was an endless blue, and the sea that wine-dark colour we have not yet managed to translate from the Greek. In spite of the seascapes over towards the islands, it was the mainland views that held us, starting up towards the Sound of Sleat and the low hills before Loch Alsh, and sweeping in a great purple offering east and southwards to Ardnamurchan and beyond to Caliach Point, in Mull, with ranges away inland to the Grampian Hills. In the sea, Muck and Coll were mere foreground fragments. The man who preaches a sermon yonder has a rich start in the samples of God's handiwork under the eye.

The man who preached the sermon was as unusual as his parish. The Reverend Mr. MacWhirter would announce the psalms from his pulpit, and then sweep out of the perch in his black robes like a bat, to huddle over the small harmonium, pounding and pedalling the uncertain melody. He was no islesman, having recently come from an industrial parish of Lanarkshire, and he was shortly to leave the Small Isles and move on.

In the meantime he was enjoying himself. Each time it was necessary for him to voyage to another of the islands to take a service there, or perform some pastoral office, he donned a white yachting cap and placed himself in the bow of the Muck launch, gulping enormous rations of sea-air as they hammered solidly through the Atlantic. Upon the glebe, which ran for many green acres about the huge manse house, he was engaged in some stock-rearing experiments, and we learned from himself of a recent hitch in this planned husbandry.

At a sale on the mainland he had bought and shipped home a stallion Highland pony, arranging also for the vet to arrive in a day or two and make the beast a gelding. In the meantime the pony had been put into a meadow occupied by the minister's mare, and while there had made unexpected use of his opportunities. In the course of nature, and long after the vet had come and finished his fell work, the mare dropped a splendid foal; and the pony was still to be seen scrutinising, perhaps with a knowing eye, this leggy pledge of his erstwhile virility.

Mr. MacWhirter had tackled the problem of his bachelor housekeeping by engaging an ex-R.N. manservant, and when we visited the manse one evening we found the pair busy at a gallant scone-baking. The results fell short of perfection, and the blae

15. RHUM SEEN BEYOND EIGG. We saw this view as we started to round the northern point of Eigg, on the left of the picture.

16. OUR LAST CAMP ON EIGG. *Seumas is on the right, and Rhum is seen in the background. We had failed to reach it the night before, and were nearly wrecked on the boulders which hide the near shore-line. The islet inshore is Eilan Thuilm.*

17. A MALLAIG KIPPERING SHED. *Cleaned herrings are impaled on rods, and hang for thirty-six hours in the smoke of oak chips. A pillar of cloud rises above the sheds, as a distant beacon to Hebridean mariners.*

scones were fed to the hens, a flock of which was developing about the door, as another stock side-line.

Our own taste in scones had again been grossly flattered by the productions of Mrs. MacDonald. Our slightly replenished purse enabled us to call for more. On each occasion we battled for the right to make a little payment. I understand this to be another of the differences which distinguish exploration in our countryside from that carried out in foreign parts. It is the custom, one reads, to haggle with the foreign native over the price to be paid, with a flurry of bidding and bargaining on both sides. The same practice is common with us, although, in the Highlands, it is the seller who is bidding down, or even refusing payment, and the purchaser who is bidding up. It is a situation often exploited by the stranger, perhaps unwittingly, and one hears of advice given: 'You musn't offer payment for anything they give you. They're very offended if you don't take it for nothing.' One would hope that the traveller with a decent appreciation of modern conditions will not go too far in applying to his case the ancient standards of hospitality.

Between the soda and the treacle scones, we were in as great a dilemma as with the scones and the pancakes at Calve. It was a ceaseless anxiety to decide which were best to eat. With all the electric ovens and aluminium girdles and fancies of to-day, how many people know how to bake scones like these? One morning we got the biscuit tin filled for the last time, and packed for an afternoon departure.

Rhum was the next stop, and its mere appearance on our schedule meant the making of a little piece of history. Our best route there was to be northwards up the east coast of Eigg, and then out north-west and straight up Loch Scresort, the port where the only houses lay. The wind had gone more northerly too, but we hoped that this would die.

No one had seen us arrive in Eigg, and there was no one to watch us go. We paddled away out through the familiar channel between the two perches north of the harbour, came round the huddle of reefs off Rudha na Crannaig, and kept into the shore for the pull up the coast. There was plenty of shelter inshore, for the cliffs fall sheer almost to the sea, the only shore at most points being mere rock debris weathered and fallen off the face. Over this face, nearly a thousand feet high for most of its length, spout a succession of waterfalls, trailing downwards like moving lace. They are merely the normal hill burns, which start in the high wet ground, and on their way to the sea suddenly lose their footing and make the endless drop. In an east wind they fold back on themselves as they reach the cliff edge, and are scattered back inland upon the grass of the plateau, where they rise to gather in their little moor channel and struggle seawards vainly again. This day the wind was from the other direction, but it was strong enough to search down over the precipices to our level, promising a harder greeting when we should leave the lee.

The shore bent away eventually towards the north-west and into the wind's eye. A muffled belt appeared ahead like a harbour bar, streaming free past the end of Eigg through the water where we were going. We drove into it, and knew we were in real weather again. There was a sudden chill in the late September wind too, which even the heat of our effort could not thaw. We bent and dipped to a long grind to clear the north end of Eigg and reach the Sound of Rhum. There were two miles to cover, and they took us over two hours.

It was necessary that we should reach Rhum, and land and stay on it. It is an island with a dark history, and its name had followed us like a challenge since we had left the Crinan Canal. 'You won't be landing on Rhum anyway?' we had been repeatedly told. 'They don't allow anybody on the island.' This we had heard so often that we had come to reply at last that, if we got nowhere else, we should certainly land on Rhum.

The whole island is preserved as a private estate, and it is official information to yachtsmen, mountaineers, geologists, as well as mere travellers and tourists, that visitors are not encouraged. It is a phrase which can cover a variety of discouraging practices, and its modern story starts badly with the undeniable episode of the Clearances in the eighteen-twenties, when the four hundred inhabitants were evicted in a body, and shipped to somewhere overseas. Memories are alive, and I judge them authentic, of the terrors of that time. One can pore with pleasure over the scale-map of the island, peppered with place-names, and discern something of the love with which a happy community dowered in apt descriptive Gaelic names their peaks and passes, the seal rocks and the cave bays, the upland lochs and mosses, the sea and inland cliffs, the

THE FORBIDDEN ISLAND

rivers, the burns, the braes. All this in a noble, small land-mass in the sea, six miles square, with a tumultuous skyline.

It is not that Rhum has no modern challengers. The adjacent townships and villages, on isle and mainland, seethe with stories of indignation and reprisals. Raids on the deer are frequent, although perhaps more frequent in story than in performance. There are those in Mallaig who will claim, unofficially, to have seen poached stags unloaded from boats returned after a Rhum foray. It is an unhappy atmosphere, mingling banditry and restriction. And it exists. We had pledged ourselves, in print and to a countless acquaintance, to land and spy out this strange land, and to report. It was utterly essential that we should reach Rhum.

At the time of which we speak, however, it was becoming doubtful if the hour for the visit had arrived. Beyond the north point of Eigg we had another seven miles of open water to face, and we had seldom seen water so open and gaping. The wind was coming hard from the direction of Loch Scresort, Rhum's only harbour, and from the whole Atlantic, which was situated just round the corner. It brought not only the broken waves which rode the main mass of the water, but also the waves which it lifted from the sea and flung at us. Eigg fell away on our left as we pulled on. To stop paddling meant the losing of a great deal of way, so that it was impossible to bale, and the canoes were filling uncomfortably. A point came when we ceased to make headway at all. About two miles out from Eigg we simply sat, flailing on at the sea, and making no forward progress. The wind had no pity, and felt as if it would blow for ever. Very little more of this and we should be too tired to keep control. So we did what we had never yet done on the trip—turned round about and ran for where we had come from.

The wind and seas took us swiftly towards the shore. We surf-rode as we chose. A shout back and forward between us settled for a landing-place on the north-west, the nearest shore of Eigg, so that our next stage back towards Rhum would be the shortest possible distance. Nearer the shore, we picked up the small island called Eilan Thuilm, and aimed to land behind it, to lessen the onrush which would bear us heavily on the rocks. We worked strenuously towards this lee, baling hard at intervals, to lighten the load of the canoes and keep them from damage by reducing the solid weight which would strike. Because it was clear that we were going to strike, and that heavily.

Nearer in, we saw that the shore was large boulders, and surf was spouting among them. It was too late to back out and try another place. Slowing down as much as we dared by the dangerous process of back-paddling, we struck. I rested for a moment on a round brown boulder which ran suddenly dry and punched me jarring on the thighs through the slats and fabric of my keel. I was half-way out and up to the waist, in the hope of running the canoe up among the rocks, when the next wave took us both, canoe and me. I lost it, and went bundling up among the boulders, got to my feet some yards on, and floundered, battering my bare feet, grabbing after the painter. I got it before the next wave, and we went in this time hand in hand, as it were, bumping painfully; myself wincing over my own shin-bones, and agonising as the canoe's ribs cracked. Eventually the canoe wedged close inshore, and, water-filled, would not be moved even by the successive waves which submerged us. Seumas, who had made a more adept if not a drier landing, splashed through to heave us both ashore, myself and canoe. Presently the paddle also came in.

At this stage we were certain that the trip was finished. In skin and ribs the canoes had taken such a damaging that they should have been unrepairable. And we were so soused and bruised ourselves as to delay the post-mortem until the morning. There was a strip of green here, good camping site save for the endless wind to which it was exposed, and we tented up, managing to build a low wind-break of stones round our walls before the darkness came down.

A miraculous healing fell upon us all during the night. A cold sunlight washing the tent roof woke us, and we stretched, feeling no more than surface wounding. A sortie to the canoes revealed a similar condition. By a freak of their fragile strength they had no ribs sprung and no rents, although we could still hear, knelling in our ears from the time of the landing, the sounds with which they had crashed ashore, tossing and crunching like flotsam tea-chests. One or two holes punched in the fabric were the only damage we could find, although a survey of the shore at low tide showed almost every rock in sight smeared with the blue paint rasped from our keels, to say nothing of other blotches we fancied could be our blood. A few strips of sticking-plaster patched up our ocean-going craft and ourselves, and we began to get ready again for the attempt on Rhum.

It was the same kind of day; perhaps a little slacker in the wind, but bitter cold, with a steep sea making ashore and promising a soaking launch. We were now beginning to reckon exposure among our potential handicaps. Yesterday had shown that, with the wind northerly, the heat of paddling was not enough to eliminate over very many hours the fangs of the wind, nor could our bodies be sure of warming up to a tolerable temperature the inevitable shipped water in which we sat. So we tried a new launching trick in the hope of getting dry away. Normally we pushed off straight into shore breakers, wading until we had two feet of depth, slipping aboard and sitting, to paddle out through the broken water. The essential pause when the canoe was taking our weight meant a brief loss of headway and control, and by the time the canoe was driving well offshore the cockpit had swallowed some inches of water, a nucleus of which remained for the rest of the day.

For to-day's launch we donned bonnets and oilskins against the wind. Running the canoes out through the nearest shallows, we shielded the cockpits with the skirts of our oilskins against the first few breakers. Then, each man watching for his wave lull, we stepped in and paddled off standing up, so that the canoes were never halted, and we hitched and jumped them over the waves rather than through them, until fairly into the Sound. Only then did we take time to get squeezed down into the sitting position, finding negligible water there compared with our normal intake. This is perhaps an advanced form of canoe handling. We used it several times later in similar conditions, finding that our bare feet planted on the canoe bottom gave us an enormously stronger and more urgent control of balance, in spite of the much higher centre of gravity in the standing position.

And then the long slog to Rhum, although we were inside the grand pillared entrance of Loch Scresort before we could feel assured that the wind would not beat us back. Every mile of the seven took us a full half-hour, heads down and eyes three-quarters shut. Only when we were well in towards the loch end could we look up, in the lee, and see round. Ahead was Kinloch Castle, a red sandstone pile, distinguished among fine trees, with a hamlet scattering of houses about. We turned aside and landed below a small plantation of trees which promised camping shelter, splashing ashore with more noise than we were used to making, and intoning 'Rhum, Rhum! Here we come!' or some such exuberance.

This time we brought up the canoes and laid them in a V to enclose the tent. A stag came up to the fence and leaned his Royal head over, coughing at us in the bronchial signal of the rut. He came to visit us frequently in the next hours.

A large man, in tweeds, with a gun and two dogs, arrived scrambling round a shore path and came over towards us. As we continued with the arrangement of our camp site, there was a short conversation:

'Have you got permission to land here?'

'Yes.'

'Who from?'

'Ourselves!'

It was an almost casual opening, but complete. In the stiff ensuing silence Seumas and I conversed normally as we unpacked. There was an adjacent throat-clearing and—

'You can't stay here without permission.'

'We're here!'

'You'll need permission!'

'We're staying!'

Our contribution to this was of an offhand character. The tent was now out of its bundle and the pole was assembling. The visitor drew nearer.

'You'll have to see Lady Bullough before you put that tent up. Just leave the tent here and come to see Lady Bullough.'

'The tent is going up!' This was said with some volume, and the tones may well have reached the castle. Short as the conversation was, it took place at a backcloth which was the rising tent. Its off-white weathered shape was already erect and pegged. Now we ripped out our bundles with the dry clothes and towels, and, as if the man with the gun had no existence, we stripped and dried ourselves upon the grass, standing and flexing and towelling with the shiver of cold delight this moment always gave us. It was a naked insult, and on the horizon of our casual view—for we didn't even look at him—we could see the man's face flame as red as the sunset. This was from no physical embarrassment, but

THE FORBIDDEN ISLAND

because he was ignored—treated like a paid convenience, a situation with which, in his present service, he was doubtless familiar. There was a sense, indeed, in which we pitied the man for our behaviour. He was a Highlander, but he was in the wrong setting, and we were at no pains to hide our contempt. In a moment or two we were kilted and clothed and well shod, glowing against the chill of the night. As we started to make a meal, the man with the gun and the dogs went off by the way they had come.

Some time later he was back, with a new opening:
'Would you gentlemen like to come and see Lady Bullough?'
'Certainly! We should very much like to see Lady Bullough.'

Our little procession wound round to the head of the loch, and we chatted on such topics as might be allowed to be of common interest. The island well knew of our voyage, and, indeed, of our intention to make Rhum a port of call. But the conversation was heavy with an overlay of the proprietorial principle, that no part of this island moor could under any circumstances offer a welcome, or perhaps even a foothold, to the visitor.

At one point, our guide related, pathetically ingratiating:
'When you were paddling up the loch this evening Lady Bullough phoned me down and said: "There are poachers in the loch. Don't allow them to land!" And I said: "These aren't poachers. They're sports." "Well," she said, "they musn't land anyway!" But I said . . .'

Arrived at the castle, our guide went in to announce us. He was back soon, with apologies.

'Lady Bullough is very sorry, she can't see you now. But you have her permission to camp on the island, and we have to give you a haunch of venison with her compliments.'

We accepted the explanation, and the promise of the tribute, gravely, and strolled off about our business upon the forbidden ground. Not another hint of hostility came into the air again, although we have not heard that subsequent excursions have fared as lavishly. We were indeed received with kindness on all sides, as if the people of the place were relieved to be able to break away from a forbidding routine. In one of the houses we were invited to a sumptuous supper of roast venison, and the lady of the house prepared a packet of sandwiches to take us over the

Sound of Sleat on the next day. For a long time we retained the memory of a child of this house—a girl at least twelve years of age, yet so unused to new faces on this desert island that she crouched all the evening shyly behind a chair, peeping and giggling like a four-year-old.

Crossing a courtyard in the late darkness, we came on an unforgettable scene. Lamplight streamed from a deep door, and we stepped into a butcher's workshop. Four stags, the day's kill, were being dismembered by a group of young Skyemen, who went at the job with bloody hands, making enormous shadows on the walls. As we watched them, they ripped the venison apart— the heads with their antlers on a side bench, the carcasses slung up to chained hooks, the hides off like cheese-cloth, and the knives and saws going with inhuman skill. These were apparently gillies brought to the island for the shooting season. It was a vivid picture—a strong and simple scene—one to put on canvas.

There is a post office on the island, although the traffic is trifling. It was a Cockney voice which served us here—indeed, we discovered only one Gaelic speaker among the two dozen or so of permanent residents. He was the chief stalker, and he had little opportunity of using his native language. While the postmistress went into the rear premises for some telegraph forms, we took from the counter the dated franking stamp and imprinted it plentifully upon our log, so as to authenticate our visit. And, oddly, this landing and camping affair of ours still seems to be most rare. We also stamped the backs of our wrists, and even, I think, our palms, with 'Isle of Rhum'.

Having landed, there was nothing else to be done here. We had hoped to include also in our Small Isles circuit a visit to Canna, lying still farther to the west, but decided to abandon this in favour of a push north, via Mallaig. Accordingly we were packing by early morning, with the wind still westerly, and fresher than we cared to have it. Our course was to be due east to Mallaig, and this twenty-mile passage would be the longest yet in open water, with only a passing glance, midway, at the shore of Sleat, in Skye. Anyway, the wind was right for us, and we packed. Also, we took delivery ceremoniously of the haunch of venison. It weighed twenty-six pounds, professionally bagged and sewn, and it dangerously upset all our stowage technique.

Rather than refuse it on any ground of sailing safety, we should have abandoned our most needful possessions. After a deal of experiment, however, we lashed the mighty thing on the top of Seumas's stern section, with the shank bone pointing aft, and the massed meat of the haunch snugging up to the small of his back. I took over bundles of his stuff to spread out the weight, and in this way we got trimmed and afloat at last.

On the way out of Loch Scresort towards the east we had enough smooth water to see how Seumas was riding. He was truly weighted, with precariously little free-board left; and this persuaded us not to use the sails, although we were to have the wind with us. There was a fine wind, too, for the direction we were taking. But paddling would have to do. Sailing, although giving us a good deal more speed and ease, would have forced the freighted canoe much too low.

It was a six-hour pull at the paddles, in heavy sea all the way. Once clear of the Rhum coast there was no shelter whatever, and we took more water aboard than normal because the sterns were too heavy to come up fast to the following sea. However, the venison was a good breakwater on Seumas's poop, and it was well brined before we had gone far. It was not a passage which could be forced. We went on at our own pace, stopping the paddles for not more than five minutes in the six hours. It was too cold, indeed, to stop, and much rain blashed in showers that looked like smoke columns as they came up astern, and felt like lances.

We had hoped to encounter on the way some of the great fleet of steam herring drifters then fishing out of Mallaig, many of whose crews we knew. But for four-fifths of the way there were none in sight, and that for a reason which was later to cause us modestly to preen. The weather was too bad for them! Of course, we had the wind more or less astern. At no point of the passage could we conceivably have turned round and attempted to go back. Only one vessel passed us on the route. It was later than our half-way stage, when we seemed to be close to the Point of Sleat, Skye's most southerly mark, and felt a sense of comfort that here was a solid place to make for if things should get worse. The white houses of Aird were quite clear in the occasional sunshine. Then the upper works of a small ship appeared between us and the land. She was throwing water over her mast, but, what made for more unease, she was hull down, which meant that the land beyond her was even miles away.

For the second part of the trip we needed no compass, as the great white pillar of smoke rising above Mallaig fattened out of the sea ahead, and we watched it grow for ten miles, until the roofs of the high kippering sheds appeared, where it comes from. When we were so far past the Point of Sleat that we could no longer see it on our left without turning to look, we had a few miles only to go. They were long, but they passed.

A mile or two off Mallaig we could see the houses and the harbour easily. One or two herring drifters came out—the only ones, we learned later, to make a fishing that day—and turned south-west for the Coll banks. This pointed them into the weather, so that they shortly looked like Shetland sea-ponies, throwing ragged manes of spray out of their eyes, and bucking skittishly. Soon we were near enough to see people on the pier, and to be seen ourselves. Nearing still, we watched the whole silent and busy pantomime of arrival excitement—the pointed arms, the beckonings and runnings, the training and passing of binoculars, the climbings on to railway wagons—until the outer quay wall was a black spectating mass, which moved with us shouting round the end of the pier. The mass fringed the harbour edge with our progress all the way, and eventually milled below the end of the road to watch us bump ashore. Then the active fragments sprayed off from the edges and ran towards us, and they were men and boys helping to lift us and our canoes ashore. This was a kind welcome, the more so because the people had dignity themselves. As we chatted and chaffed with them in a first passage of words, the news spread back that we had come from Rhum, and this was satisfying in the highest degree, being both a joke and a wonder as well. As the crowd continued to grow and press around, we left the canoes to them at last and slipped off to see to our livelihood at the post office.

Here we found a certain shyness, as we sent off our Press wires, for the ladies of the official service had urged our arrival, and here we were! Nor were we prepared to be fobbed off, as was their ruse, by being attended at the grill by the junior staff. We had Mrs. Watt, the postmistress, and her daughter Ethel haled from the back premises to answer for themselves, and there was a hilarious session of mock-complaint and counter-charge, until passers-by came in to discover what the laughter was about, and another concourse formed. One thing, as the saying goes, led to another, to such effect that we were shortly installed in the parlour of the Watts' house, which was handily affixed to the post office. Here, still in our tattered and salt-bleached paddling flimsies, we went at a substantial tea, and held occasional court as friendly heads came round the door incessantly. Everybody, I think, felt better after this.

CHAPTER XIII

THE HIGHLAND PROBLEM

>Laughter was easy yonder!
>   Life was alive to win.
>Yesterday's tale was wonder,
>Albyn was light and thunder,
>   Rich in my clan and kin.
>
>Whether I'm leal or lying,
>   Life at the start, or done—
>To-day has a tale of dying,
>Doom, and no glory nor crying,
>   Sunset without the sun.

THE Highland problem is the oldest problem in Scotland. The attempt to solve it has always been abandoned by those whom it has defeated, and the story spread that the place is not worth having and saving anyway. In the days when physical conquest was the mode of achieving economic unity, many a sour-grapes despatch went back to Rome by the military post from the Wall. It was doubtless mentioned on all sides that the country was poor and barren, and the people shiftless and lazy—although, as the serving Roman would admit, they kept the legions on the run.

It has been easy, in the nineteen centuries which have passed, to put the same tale about, and to have it believed. The eagerness of the world to believe it is worth a study in itself. Samuel Johnson, speaking on the subject of the Highlands, committed one of the greatest howlers in European letters, and his reputation has suffered not a whit. The Highlander has never been in charge of the organs of civilised opinion, and, in any case, he has never been asked for evidence. Giving the Highland dog a bad name has long been a sport nearer home. 'Wolves and wild boars' was James VI's description of his Hebridean subjects. A hundred years later, here is a Sheriff-Clerk of Inverness-shire writing to the Privy Council and telling of the people of the Highlands and Isles as 'infested with poverty and idleness'.

THE HIGHLAND PROBLEM 133

There must have been some virtue there too, and energy. Very shortly afterwards, in 1745, a few thousands of them emerged from their wilderness and blitz-krieged a dazzling way southward, to stagger England to the vitals. It is the only army I know of in well-recorded history of which no atrocity stories are told.

A straight line drawn from a spot twenty miles north of Glasgow to one twenty miles north of Aberdeen will cut Scotland in half. Broadly speaking, everything to the north and west of this line is in the Highlands; and, the farther west, the more Highland. In the western sea there is a spray of islands, the Hebrides, close on a hundred of them inhabited. Only at one or two short periods of recorded history have the Highlands moved sweetly along with the rest of Scotland in a progressive picture of a homogeneous nation. In the basic sense, Scotland is an economic unity. The Highland satellites still find their orbit in the administrative centre of Scotland, and nowhere else. But in every other sense the apartness of the Highlands is complete. They cannot, by their own efforts, fit into the modern industrial state: they never could: and the State is too busy to find a berth for them: it always has been. This is the Highland problem.

Nevertheless, the Highlander has been able to find for himself an ample life. He has a fertile land. Upon it—apart from the stony uplands—he used to feed a multitude of cattle, and could still do so. There is a mildness along the western coasts, brought by the Gulf Stream: or rather by its offshoot, the North Atlantic Drift, whose eternal task is to import to this spot the warm sea-climate of Florida. Frost and snow seldom lie in the islands, nor in the rich alluvial valleys of the mainland. High winds and a heavy rainfall are frequent, but the harvests are always brought in. Not until 1950 did anything come of endless efforts to create an asset out of the high rainfall for the benefit of the Highland people themselves. In that year started the first of the great water-power schemes of the North of Scotland Hydro-Electric Board. It seems likely that a harnessing of the winds will follow after. And if tides can also be turned to power for the switching on, there are tides and races ready for the experiment.

The fertility of the Highlands is an old story. Only the absence of a reliable transport system on land and sea has kept this benign productivity on a freak and amateur basis. The

Highlands share with the rest of Scotland in enjoying the acceptance of the description 'Scotch' as a universal indication of superior quality—herring, salmon, beef, honey, wool, potatoes, mutton, lobsters, shell-fish, whisky, bacon, tomatoes. In the world markets, the adjective 'Scotch' applied to these items and to many more means invariably a price higher than the market average. The word means quality.

MacKenzie, in his *A Hundred Years in the Highlands*, tells of luxurious growths in his remarkable garden. We ourselves spoke to men who had seen peaches growing in the open air in Rhum. Canna, Islay, and others of the islands can grow early potatoes as early and as good as the southern fields. During our visit to Muck they had a hay crop of over two tons to the acre. Much of the soil appears to have great potential, responding richly when well limed and nourished with manures. The wind is the chief enemy, burning the unprotected growths with its salt content; and the development of tree belts should be a matter for early investigation. In sheltered gardens and parklands the growth is prodigious. Palms are comfortable immigrants. Tomatoes are open-air plants. We saw fruit trees at Scallasdale whose branches had had to be supported as the weight of fruit became insupportable by the tree trunks themselves, and indeed eventually broke off by their own exuberance. Other garden and wild fruits blacken their bushes in the season, and have undoubtedly a commercial significance.

The wealth of the place, the fertility, the richness that could ensue in the provision of good eating and plenishing for modern man, is by no means an empty speculation. To apply to the potential energy of the soil all the modern techniques of agriculture and chemistry would be a fair and rewarding sight. But the result would not be novel. At one time the wilderness did indeed blossom like the rose—although, on present-day standards, perhaps it was like the wild rose. Those who find some difficulty in conceding the possibilities of a re-established cattle industry might well remember that this was at one time a great cash and export trade. At one cattle fair in Crieff in 1723 more than thirty thousand guineas in ready money were paid over, mainly by English dealers. The 'Roast Beef of Old England' was a Highland tale, and a well-paying one at that. I find it hard to believe, following these Argentinian-fed post-war years, that a similar gathering in Crieff would not bring the English dealers flocking with ready guineas.

It is the sight of the vast derelict tracts of the modern Highlands, with their ruined homesteads, bracken-covered pastures and soured and bogged meadows, which create the ready illusion that these places were always the scenes of a doleful and meagre living standard, from which emigration was a welcome rescue. It would be as valid to assume, from the sight of the ruined Parthenon, that ancient Athens boasted nothing better than a tumbledown and roofless culture.

The cause of the Highland problem, and its ills, is that every trend and event of its modern life has been out of timing, and it has been nobody's business to set it right. When the wreck of the Forty-five Rising threw down all the geographical barriers, it was the task of Government to nurse this delicate area, with its almost prehistoric social structure, out of its apartness and into the growing modern society in which it could have played so potent a part. But the Government of the United Kingdom had other tasks on its hands. It found itself able to call on the Highlanders, but not on the Highlands. They were to become a mere quarry for the raw material of pioneering and soldiery. And it was to be the task of the Highlander to play a great part in the shaping of the New World, while at the same time his community was debarred from growing into rhythm with the expanding Britain to which it belonged.

You cannot, however, man a New World without leaving gaps in the defences of the Old. The traditional Highland way of life upon the land was a patriarchal system, and so it remains. It makes little difference to the case—or to the Highlander—if the landlord is an individual, or the State. After the Forty-five, few clan chiefs remained as landlords. They suffered proscription; or they cut themselves off, by entering into English society. In this way or that, they were leaders permanently lost to a community which was badly in need of leadership. The Highlander answered this deprivation by imposing upon himself the severest discipline of Calvinism, at a time when the rest of Christendom was progressively adopting more liberal doctrines.

The Highlands were further caught out of stride by the sudden onset of the Industrial Age at their back door. It was in the south-west of Scotland on the Clyde, that the machine started first to take over from man, and many of the Highlanders fled from their forgotten lands to a scene in which society was at least interested. At the same time, the vacuum left by the lost chief was being filled, on a number of estates, by the arrival of wealthy landowners, who had purchased the estates, perhaps for sporting or picturesque reasons, but were disposed to spend money on amenities. This was the benevolent modern version of the protecting clan chief, and the Highlander welcomed it. If he was not to move with the times, at least he might as well be comfortable where he sat. It was a shrewd enough instinct, for in the recent Highland history, proprietors have spent more development money on their estates than the Government. This is not to make a case for those proprietors who have been permitted to buy land and to shed the people from off it. These, always to be execrated for their own sake, are the mere proof that the State had abandoned the Highlands. Such expenditure as had been forced from it was mere scratching of the surface; a grant for a piece of road here, a pier there. Britain's Highland policy has been one of relief doles, not capital investment.

By another costly act of ill-timing, the work of the romantic writers, who "discovered" the Highlands after the Jacobite barriers fell, tended to keep the place forced back into its archaic shell. It became overdosed with historical curiosity. The result was that too early a start was made with a tourist movement, before, as it were, a modern shape of the land was well laid. It was the wrong kind of tourism—a moneyed, shooting, antlers-in-the-great-hall, piper-on-the-terrace tourism. Hence much energy went to the creation of vast hotels and shooting lodges, and the development of sporting estates, with fatal diversions into the easily learned techniques of gillies, stalkers, gamekeepers, and piper-valets. This has caused the slow growth of what could be a most lucrative modern tourist industry, due to the long-held belief in the Highlands that the tourist is a millionaire, with excessive expectations in the matters of food, service, and sanitation.

The special blight of the romantic school of writing has been that it denied the countryside any present-day significance, and the people any forward-looking way of thought. A tourist policy for the Highlands must work hard now to combat the determined bid which the romantics have made for over a

18. THE FRINGES OF ARDTOE HAMLET. Rhum rises like the fore-sight of a rifle above Eigg as the back-sight, across the Sound of Eigg, which we traversed. Ardtoe is fourteen miles from the end of the Ardnamurchan peninsula. The crofter's bay is seen in 'tramps' near his small arable patches, and his boat, which reaps a second harvest from the sea, is ashore on the right.

19. PEAT-CUTTING IN SKYE. *Communal work is needed to win the winter fuel. When there is no road near by, as there is here, peats are carried home on the Highlanders' shoulders.*

hundred and fifty years to suggest that the land is even emptier than is the case. Ruined castles, picturesque and empty landscapes, an occasional elderly shepherd or crofter figure mumbling some clan legend, is all that has been permitted to appear. Many a current—and I hope a rapidly tarnishing—reputation has been made on a stock collection of worn old yarns, strung together in a volume with photographs. 'Didn't So-and-so visit the island last year?' we asked of one woman, mentioning a renowned writer of this school. 'Yes,' she agreed heavily, with terrible patience. 'He was here looking for fairy tales!' This was an island which was plainly dying because of the mere matter of communications, whose solution was one of the earliest triumphs of the modern age everywhere else. There was no way of assuring regular transport to the mainland and south for the wealth of lobsters they could catch. And all other development was subject to the same frustration. Yet among this present decay a self-styled journalist was peddling his ill-timed antiquarianism. Those who charge that the Highlander lives in the past had better make sure that they mean the Highlander himself, and not his accepted interpreters.

The pictures, the scenic photographs, the postcards, which illustrate these romantic scenes, are a plague in themselves of a special sort. Almost without exception they portray an empty landscape. Broken-down sheilings, the empty glen, the castle on the sea-cliff—these are the stock-in-trade of the cameraman in the Highlands. We differ from all other peoples in this, that we portray as a tourist inducement, not an active and lively peopled country, but an empty one. Elsewhere, the boasted charm of the foreign scene lies in its crowded mart, busy streets and cafés, rural pursuits and festivals, its peasant types, its craftsmen. Scotland's habit has been to display itself as a land without Scots. Indeed, without life. I have watched one of the best-known scenic photographers in Scotland drive a straying flock of sheep out of the foreground of his picture, lest it should disturb the barren composition.

The Highlands are not deserted. But over great tracts they are empty, with the bleakness of a neglected asset. We have seen that the Highlands and Isles occupy one half of the land area of Scotland. To the south of the Highland line live close on five million people. To the north live fewer than three hundred thousand Highlanders. It is a pitiful total: and yet, thinking of the Highland problem, it is a miracle that there are people there at all. Our canoe voyage lay among the more remote fringes, far from the bigger centres of population. In the Highlands there are many small towns, some of them prosperous. From none of these has come any leadership for the rural areas, nor for the Highlands as a whole. The Highlander of the countryside—of the crofting and fishing fringes—lives on a constant pendulum of the gluts and slumps which bedevil the primary producer in any unprotected economic system. He is further shackled through the almost certain failure of any production project— be it fruit-growing, shellfish-gathering, lobster-fishing, or any other of the ventures in quality perishables which would be highly profitable in another place with similar resources—because of the lack of any reliable form of communications or transport. The steamer cannot call in certain weather because of the lack of a pier; or there is no road across the sodden bog; or there is no telephone with which to make a transaction. I anchored in a yacht in the lovely isle of Canna a year or two after the war, and went ashore in the evening to telephone to Edinburgh. The postmistress worked vigorously to connect me, and when she failed I came ashore again in the morning, when we tried again. At last I got through, and carried out a faint and tinny conversation across the paltry distance. The postmistress regarded this as a feat on the part of her installation. It was the first time for two days that anyone had been able to talk beyond Mallaig. My business was private and might well have waited. In the bay, however, were six or eight herring boats which had come to anchor the morning before with their catches. They had hoped to discover by telephone which was the likeliest market for their herring. And, trying for hours, they had failed; eventually having to scramble the catches aboard one or two of the vessels and send them speculatively to ports where there might be a market. It seemed to me an illustration of the commercial need for good communications in these parts, quite apart from the social and tourist needs.

Transport, the physical moving of men and things from place to place, is a fantastic ordeal and difficulty. The existing systems are in no way adequate to the needs of the community or its visitors, and the burdens of its oncost are hard to believe. When we were at Tobermory, the transfer of live stock by steamer to the sales at Oban, twenty-five miles away, cost five per cent. of what the stock might be expected to realise at the sale. The whole price of one sheep out of twenty went to pay the transport for the score. To realise the price of nineteen cows, a farmer had to rear and feed another one to pay for the transport alone.

Because of such incidents, which are the substance of his daily life, the chief virtue of the Highlander on his own ground is patience. It is a patience born of facing, not only the raw end of every modern development, but of endless weather, driving with a ceaseless wind and a heavy winter rain under the lintels of his mind. He has paced himself to his difficulties, and shows little visible reaction to failure or success, in himself or others. Denied the great part of contemporary amenity, he has taken refuge from contemporary excitements by seeing himself as a part of a long and noble tradition, and by being little moved to action by day-to-day details. If this be laziness—the description most normally applied by his critics—it is a quality whose adoption might lead to more mental ease in other spheres.

One disadvantage of his leaning on tradition is that the Gael always puts himself at the hinder end of his own history, and would have you believe that there is nothing to come after. Having suffered at the hands of the modern world, and seeing little future for his people as a community, he will rather bemoan the past than tempt Providence by hopeful forecasts of the future. He is especially wary of tempting Providence. This is the origin of the phrase that came word-perfect and unanimously from so many different lips: 'It's too late in the year', in describing our own trip. It is his normal mode to quell optimism—and who, knowing the history of the Gael, will blame him for the trick at this stage in his career. Not that he lost faith in himself, as an individual. Far from it. But he ceased to dare hope for a future for his race, as a factor in the world community. 'The old people are all away,' the elderly Gael will say grudgingly. He means merely that most of his own generation have gone, and that they were the best of their kind. That is why, in spite of the well-developed sense of social responsibility which makes him the kindly succourer of the distressed neighbour and the hospitable host to the stranger, he will with infinite reluctance take part in any move of communal organisation to save himself.

The Highlander of the present day, marvellously adaptable to the world in which he finds himself, is ceaselessly conscious of the world from which he comes. He has a sure knowledge of his roots and their worth. It is a point well made in two very different books published within the past few years. Each is autobiographical, dealing with the life of a young child growing up in Britain in the eighteen-eighties. In *Lark Rise to Candleford*, Flora Thompson tells of her girlhood in rural Oxfordshire; while in *The Former Days*, Dr. Norman MacLean describes his boyhood in Skye, at precisely the same period of history. The rural folk of the English book are rustics, with a hazy recollection of their local lore and little awareness of the manner and persons of even their grandparents. The Skye book, on the other hand, is a description of a civilisation, well recorded in its own mind with the events which have shaped it, and conscious of the men and the events it comes from.

The clan sentiments go deep, and they are more than sentimental. 'Where do you come from?' is one of the first questions asked of a town Scot by another, for the interest is real in the place of origin. I myself find great pleasure in reading in country papers the names of football, shinty and cricket games, and seeing how the unexpected clan names of that district reel off for the modern fray.

In a certain sense, this continuing communal instinct of the Highlander, this habit of responsibility towards his own community, is his handicap. In the small villages and hamlets there is a strenuous reluctance to take any hand in altering the habits and social practices. It takes the form of a diffidence to be first in the doing of anything—to try the new season's potatoes, to plant a new crop. It is a relic of the time when the man who stepped aside from the close-knit pattern of the village or clan might endanger the whole community. We had a friend in one of the Hebridean islands who decided to plant early potatoes, in the belief that they would grow well enough to be put on the market even before the Ayrshire crop. His neighbours denounced the project as foolhardy and doomed, and when he persisted, ploughing and planting the seed in February, they used to come along to his field fence and laugh at him. The first year the thing was an amazing success; and it was known to be a success, with the bags of earlies going away by the steamer before the Ayrshires were on the market, and the huge price he got per ton well known to the whole place. On each succeeding year of the venture it was a similar success. But persistently they came along to laugh at his efforts, and the venture remained a local joke, to be dismissed with something of a sneer as the greedy impudence of an incomer. It is a savage trait, this condemnation of newness; but it speaks with terrible clarity of communities elbowed out of the main stream of national progress, and forced to retreat to the last wall of their crude securities. It is tragic to note that this is the first characteristic of the Highlander to be lost when he is away from his native soil. It drops from him once he is over the Highland line. I believe that over the years the pressure towards emigration has come not so much from a desire to escape from adverse economic conditions, as to quit the inhibiting social discipline of the ancient style of life.

The fell word Emigration brings the question to the point of its special curse. It is certain that no part of Europe has suffered the depopulating blight of the Highlands. Even in Ireland, with its great man-power losses of the nineteenth century, the movement had a different quality. Ireland has no great industrial centres eating its landward fat. The Irish countryside is still well carpeted with population; events did not unman it, as with us, by whole islands and parishes at a time.

Long back into the records of our history, the Highlander has been venturing forth upon the world in search of fortune; long after his present injustices are righted, and his citizenship restored, individuals among him will go the same road—and good luck to them. But these are not the examples which come to the mind at the thought of Highland emigration and depopulation. After the failure of the Forty-five, the Highlander embraced failure to himself as his whole fate. By complete clans and tribes, the exodus started and went on; they were swallowed up in the currents of the world, while the springs of life in the native places they had left slowed to a trickle. The effect of their prodigious pioneering in the new worlds has been amply recorded. They navigated rivers and tamed and bridged and harnessed them. They drained the swamps, cleared or planted the forests, broke the soil and made it abundant. They built cities and camps, poured out their lore and their laughter, sent herds and flocks widespread over virgin lands to the Glory of God and the nobility of man. In these two centuries they made themselves for ever a world people, as they had in medieval times made themselves a European people. Forced into conflict with the new world, they mastered and shaped it. At their backs, in its turn, the land they had left became a new wilderness. And it is to this, to the home of such a people, that the wise have been pointing this hundred years, saying that here were rivers too wide for bridging; fields too sour for planting; slopes too choked with rank growth to be worth cultivation. And these are not only opinions expressed, but lessons officially taught, to the children of those great-hearted enough to wait behind.

It will be wrong to assume that the emigrant has invariably been the most enterprising of those who heard the call—or felt the push—to go overseas. A dour grip of the ground, a sheer triumph of durability, kept numbers of the best Highlanders where they belonged. There are strong impulses still to be released in the Highlander who has held quietly to his Highland earth, and from whom little has so far been heard. But it will take a mighty national effort to do it now. Nothing of the sort has been tried. On the contrary, facilities are still being freely offered to emigrant recruiting agents from overseas to stump the country in the hope of netting some of the remaining handful. So, during the whole story, the erosion of the racial topsoil has been fostered. 'There have been no emigrations to America from this parish' writes an island minister in the old Statistical Account. By the end of the eighteenth century, then, it was already news that one parish had shipped nobody. The minister was tempting fortune with his boast: there is hardly a shipload left in that parish.

Side by side with the endless physical draining away of the stock has been the softening antiquarianism of the 'sweet-song-and-story' school of writing, glamourising the emergent Celt into an other-worldly creature, when he might, with more masculine handling, have grown up where he stood. This literary approach to our wretched hero has spread the belief that he is a hero indeed, and that everything the Highlander has done is right. Alas, and this isn't true either. He has done many wrong and foolish things, and is capable of many more. Long before the welfare state was anything like a reality he had become powerfully subsidy-minded, and it will be the major effort in his share of whatever new deal may come to him to abandon this way of thought. But, as we have seen, he always brings in his autumn harvest; he finishes his job; and, under Highland conditions, these are not ordinary feats.

As for the charge of his laziness, it must be judged in relation to the pace of life, and the object of life. One form of the charge, of which I have heard much, deals with the lethargy of the Highlander in hiring cars or boats to eager visitors, anxious to spend money. But why should he hire his car or his boat, if that is not his business? I myself feel that he should, and that he misses many chances of good will, apart from the cash, in refusing. But it is conceivable that he has not the inclination. He might be as likely, on his own winter holiday to Glasgow or Edinburgh, to jump upon the running board of a passing car, waving an offensive banknote and saying. 'Here! You might drive me round the sights of this place. Don't worry — I'll pay you!'

Outside of tradition, the great quality of the Highlander on which one can count is his willingness to experiment. At present, his experiments are confined to trivia. He is a great one for gadgets. The first place Seumas and I ever had a haircut with electric clippers was in Stornoway, and that was years before we saw the things in any of the cities. Sports and pastimes are subject to crazes which sweep communities. A shinty district will go football daft for a season, and switch back to playing shinty again. I remember how tennis once felled an area, sweeping away every other game for a summer. Or it might be pole-vaulting, or golf, or bowls, or throwing the hammer.

The one object with which the Highlander will not experiment —as yet—is his way of life. There he is warily cautious, on his guard against any slipping out of the run and pattern. The reason is plainly visible. His life till now has been a long fight for security on the land. The Crofters' Act of 1885 gave him this security, and guaranteed to him the benefits of any improvements to his holding he might make. He has what he wanted, and he will be slow to change. His mind is of such a shape that he can see no security without a hold on the land. He has gathered this security about him, and has been in no mood to step out from the shelter—although we shall be looking later at where such a step might take him. He has felt that with the wrong step he might gain the whole modern world—and lose his own soul.

CHAPTER XIV

THE HERRING FISHERS

> Thou seest, Lord, our empty nets,
>   We cast them under Heaven's face;
> Thou art, for what the fisher gets,
>   Giver and Witness of Thy grace.
> And if it fails, we ken there should
>   Be pride in our humility,
> Since we have learned of quietude
>   Within the brawling of Thy sea.

OUR pleasant progress around Mallaig, on that afternoon of our arrival, was broken by an emissary who came running to tell that 'the canoes have been damaged'. With our tail of attendants we scrambled down the lumpy beach, discovering my canoe like a fallen Roman column, her sections stricken apart from one another and the three pieces clumped on the green stones as characterless as old herring bones. Eye-witnesses were at hand to tell what had happened. In the throng of the spectators some talk had got up about the lightness of the craft, and a young man had lifted my canoe's bow in his hands high into the air, and hitched it up and down with all the weight bearing between the two extreme points. The stress had been too much for the stranding wire which held the whole structure together; it had parted with a twang, dropping the laden canoe to the beach in bits like an unstrung parcel. The unwitting saboteur had fled amid the curses of the onlookers, speaking for us.

There was an aspect in which our own indignation did not quite reach the level of that around us. The sight of the sundered hulk was able to remind us that such a separation might well have taken place on the late voyage. It was difficult to believe, for example, that the solid thumps with which we had skelped and wedged our way ashore at Eigg two days ago had been less than the strain of the rash demonstration which had broken the wire. One item of the trifling repair outfit which accompanied us was a new galvanised-wire replacement. We were able to assure everybody—including the lad who had done the damage, and was now lurking miserably on the fringes—that a repair job would be simple. But not, we determined, in the meantime. Enlisting an adequate supply of volunteers, we ran the canoes into the garage at the pier, and left them there.

At this stage initiative passed out of our hands with the arrival of a small beetling boy who shouldered through the onlookers.

'Are you looking for a place to camp? Come on here and I'll show you one.'

He led us to the east side of the bay, and into a sloping field there, behind the houses.

'How will this do? You'll get water in the burn there.'

When he had supervised the erection of the tent, he turned to the commissariat:

'What about some scones for your tea?—fresh scones! And you could do with some eggs! You get on with lighting the stoves. I'll be back in a minute.'

He was back in a minute, with a warm parcel.

'Here you are! I'll get some more in the morning. Now, what about your wet things? My mother says you've to give me everything that's wet. She'll wash them through in fresh water; otherwise you'll never get the salt out of them.'

The bustling morsel practically stripped us with his own hands, and bore the bundle away, with—

'Good night! I'll bring them back first thing in the morning.'

His name was Duncan MacDonald, one of the many of that clan who played a kindly part in our expedition. By a happy chance, he had a superb nickname, in that countryside of nicknames. It happened that his father was a professional deep-sea diver, who had in his day worked on such tasks as the building of the Forth Bridge, and the search for the Spanish treasure at Tobermory. For these exploits he was known solely by the name 'The Diver'. But for small Duncan there was an apter label, indicating at once his energy, stature, and ancestry. They called him 'The Wee Dooker'.

This black-eyed youngster emerged on several occasions during our Mallaig stay to organise us with a generous but firm hand. He summarised in more than one way the impact of an outside regional influence on the Highland character, which gives the town of Mallaig its apartness in the West. It is another of these recently created places, built about the turn of the century as a railway terminal and a centre for the herring industry. Into it have come and settled families from the east-coast fishing villages of the Moray Firth, and these truly typical easterners have mingled to make a population whose other half is of perhaps the most distinctively Celtic elements of the West Highlands. The easterners have come as coopers, herring curers, buyers and merchants, grocers and bakers. The streets resound with the Buchan dialect, and Gaelic, or the good English of the Highlands. Houses, flats, hotels, and shops have risen from the stone of the hillside, few of them attractive. But it is a place with life and an urge to be clean. Mallaig was the only place in which we had ever seen casement curtains on the windows of the tenement common stairs. Somebody pointed out to us, with pride, a pub which, in the previous summer, had been 'the bar with the biggest takings in Scotland'. During the nineteen-thirties, in seasons when the herring were running, scores and scores of boats would lie in strings off the inner pier, each boat with her nine or ten men, and most of them from the east coast. Our own Loch Fyne men used to come here in the season.

Saturday night in this town was a hearty wonder, with some rough drinking but rarely a rough word. It was a sight to see the convivial swaying cheerfully home in the darkness, across slippery moving gunwales and net-heaped decks, ill-lit, striding from boat to boat across the open harbour water as confidently as on stepping-stones in a shallow stream.

Whatever the violence of the night before, Sunday morning found them to a man making for the church on the hill above. And what men! Newly-shaved, with skins the colour of their red-tanned sails; with hair-cuts done by the engineer; every one of them in his blue reefer and best ganzie, with new shoes and hat. They would stand shoulder to shoulder in the pews, and from the pulpit they must have looked like the very men who built the whole religion. We went up the hill more than once to worship with those who came to be our special crew—the men of the *Golden Emblem*, a drifter from Gardenstown.

For one good reason and another, Mallaig held us for seventeen days, so that we changed our camp site in the sloping field more than once, to lessen the wear on the October grass. During this time the weather blew up harshly enough to keep the herring fleet in the harbour for more than half the days. We settled to a routine of writing, and were able to report on the progress of the fishing at a time when its vagaries were growing towards a pitch of national concern. Every day we were in the station at the arrival of the Glasgow train to buy a *Daily Record* and discover what of our production had made its way into the columns. We were even able to receive one or two remittances for articles, and began to feel, in a state of mind reminiscent of Tobermory, that it was pleasant to be storm-bound in Mallaig.

The place had other virtues in common with Tobermory. Dances were frequent, and we went to them all. I have never seen anything like the Mallaig quadrilles. This is danced with no less precision and correctness than in Mull, but at a galloping pace. One had the impression irresistibly that some crack Cossack dancers and tumblers were at large, with pivoting thighs of steel and spikes in their boots to preserve balance. A proper impression might be conveyed by filming an athletic troup and projecting the result at double speed. No novice dared stray near the trajectory of the experts. 'Visitation' and 'Gentlemen In' were cataclysms of rhythmic violence. The eightsome reel, regarded as an insignificant item in most Highland ballrooms, was here used as mere warming up for the major demonstrations. It was also danced at excessive speed—although in neat and perfect timing—so that the arm-swinging noted in other parts was here translated into a galvanic twitch which sent two grown humans round each other like the balls of a speed governor. The whole scene would have sent a West End producer mad, and waving a sheaf of contract forms. It was at the Mallaig dances, by the way, that we first saw the Palais Glide, just then imported from Yarmouth, Mallaig being the first place north of the Border to dance it. (Or so it was claimed.)

Participation in these ploys made many friends for us, and we had a range of invitations to tea. Characters of another sort were to be encountered in other haunts. There was, for example, a plain tearoom on the pierhead which was kept by five charming sisters. We made shameless use of this place, ordering inexpensive meals, spreading out our manuscripts and settling down to mornings of literary work. On the first occasion we patronised the premises we had not realised quite how plain was the fare available. It was strictly a tearoom. At this time there was only one other customer in the place, a nautical man of about middle age, and he was quietly drinking tea as we took our seats. The ladies in attendance were in the back premises, from which came an entrancing aroma, and indeed a noise, of frying steak and onions. A flushed sister emerged soon to take our orders.

'We'll have some of that,' we said, pointing to the source of the succulence.

'Sorry!' she said, smiling with regret. 'Only plain teas here.'

'There's nothing plain about what's going on in there,' we said. 'We'll be happy with two platefuls of that and lashings of tea and bread-and-butter.'

'It's only plain teas, I'm sorry. Bread and scones and cakes. . . .'

'We're desperate men. Two plates of yon and——'

'Oh, I'm sorry!' She was laughing ruefully. 'That's for our own breakfast. I can only give you——'

'Plain teas indeed! Who could eat a plain tea with that smell going about! How is it you get all this and we don't, eh . . .?'

'Well, we work here. . . .'

'Let us into the back shop and we'll work too.'

'We don't need you! There's plenty of ourselves. . . .'

And that was true enough. The tearoom was filling up with sisters, and we were practically holding a mass meeting, although they were not taking it very seriously.

'Listen!' we said, making what was obviously a final appeal to common decency. 'Just a wee plateful! A wee ring of onion, even. Eh?—No? . . . Well, *there's* a fine thing!' We appealed to the world at large. 'There's a fine thing! How is this for an example of Highland hospitality!'

'Hach!' said the tea-drinking man, smacking his two hands down on the table and rising to his feet. 'If it's hospitality you're looking for, you've got to carry it yourself!'

In a smooth motion he was at our side, slapping down before us two teacups which he had swept up from his own table. With a practised movement he scooped up the skirts of his big reefer and out came a bottle backwards from his hip-pocket. He dived it towards the cups, plucking the cork deftly in mid-flight. From the generous mouth gushed a glocking of liquid which looked like cold tea, but most certainly was no such thing. He stopped only when the cups were brimming, performed the same rite over a third cup, and stabled the bottle at his stern again like a bolting fox. The whole thing had taken fewer seconds than lines of type to tell.

Now, 'Slan!' he said unhurriedly, and showed us the next move by example. He emerged from his cup with a kindling eye. 'By God!' he said, in a tone of discovery, as if the stuff were new to him. 'That's better than onions yet!'

Our hospitable fellow-diner was Alastair Campbell, one of the leading citizens of the island of Soay, a small lump of croft land a mile or so from the south coast of Skye, below the Cuillin Hills. He made the passage to Mallaig at least once a week, in his rôle of mail-boat skipper and transporter of passengers and merchandise. Later, after we had finished our plain tea, we went to the harbour and held an inspection of his boat, the *Marys*. This name was one of the many engaging mysteries about our acquaintance, who revealed it to be no more than the plural of Mary, the boat having been christened after more than one. It was a smallish fishing boat of the older West Highland type, engined and converted, not too thoroughly, for the ferry run. The boat was small enough for the job, and the solitary skipper and crew man must have got many a dose of heavy weather as he went about his business. His exuberance, however, was clearly difficult to quell, and his passion to show off his island found us at once seeking a passage with him to Soay. This fell in with his own eager plans; but the time was not ripe for him to play to the full his warm double rôle of host and impresario.

'We'll leave it for another month, boys. I'll bring you over when you're on your way back south.'

'What's wrong with this time? Take us over to-day! We'll carry the canoes on board and come back in them in a few days.'

'It's too soon, though.' He was apologetic. 'I wouldn't be able to look after you right. I've still some hay to get in.'

'Don't worry about that. We'll help you with the hay.'

'Listen, boys!' He was almost the offended host. 'When you come to Soay it won't be to work!'

For plenty of reasons we never made that journey to Soay. It would have been a lively journey and sojourn, especially if there are several others in Soay like Alastair Campbell. He came to us, enraged, one day at the pier, and launched an expert tirade at the crew of Mr. T. O. M. Sopwith's yacht *Endeavour*, then sailing against the American champion in one of the fruitless British bids for the America's Cup.

'Did you hear that?—the description of yesterday's race on the wireless. My, I wonder they've the cheek to call themselves sailors at all! She's a good boat, too, that *Endeavour*, if there was them in her that could sail her. The man on the wireless was saying she was sailing with her lee rail under. What kind of sailing is that? No crew that puts a boat's rail under will ever win a race against yon Yankees! Man, I could take the engines out of the *Marys* and put sails on her and beat the *Endeavour* myself, the way they're handling her. They'll never look near the Cup this turn!'

Another seafaring novelty in the place was a motor-car ferry which had just been built by the joint enterprise of a small local shipyard and the garage where our canoes were lying. It was a craft designed to counter the difficulties involved in carrying tourist cars over to Skye. The design and all the work had been done locally, and whatever the result may have lacked in fineness, she made up for it in fitness for the job. She was built like a flat-iron, with the propeller-shaft mounted, like that of a salmon coble, in a concave channel along the keel, so that the screw actually operated at a height considerably above the normal water-level. This allowed the ferry, drawing only inches of water, to back right up the shore, drop the entire stern to form a ramp, take three cars aboard, and waddle over the Sound of Sleat to Armadale in Skye, five miles away. Commercial success had blessed this undertaking, and another possible link had been made for a Skye tour. At the time we wrote enthusiastically about this.

Another transport item to which we gave attention was the state of the road from Fort William to Mallaig, the most celebrated development theme in the whole district. The road was a narrow track for most of its length, and the inability to persuade any authority to have it surfaced and improved had baffled many generations of Mallaig folk. So great was the frustration, so typical of all Highland concerns the lack of authoritative response, so real and brooding the suspicions aroused, that it was freely believed the railway company had a vested interest in keeping the road ruinous to boost their own traffic receipts—an improbable plot, but an inevitable reasoning. We spoke to a Mallaig merchant who had alighted from his car in the darkness on a previous winter's run, to investigate an engine failure, and had stepped from his running board straight into a water-filled puddle which engulfed him to the actual waist. During that season, it was said, over sixty holiday tourists, completing the run to Mallaig, had railed their cars forty miles back to Fort William rather than face the return road trip. The surface of the road resembled, in parts, the bed of a river. The naked rock projected through ruts and loose gravel, and drove vehicles asunder. The upkeep of cars and vans in Mallaig was probably higher than in any other British community.

Although good rarely results, the people of Mallaig have a well-rehearsed system of making their transport and other problems known to anyone in a position to influence a change. No Member of Parliament, no Government official, certainly no Minister, moves in the area, on whatever innocent business, but the fiery cross goes round, and a deputation is in waiting to escort him to some local room and lay an insistent petition. One day during our stay it was learned that the M.P. for the county was on his way via Mallaig to Skye on a holiday visit. The smooth machinery went into action; delegates gathered, some of them from a distance; and (an opportunist move) I was co-opted on to this body of vigilantes.

We lay in waiting in an hotel lounge while scouts were out on the business of interception. Presently the victim was led in, as he had undoubtedly been on a score of former occasions, and on the same theme. This time he proved a receptive hearer, for he had broken an axle of his own car somewhere down the road, and had carried on with borrowed transport. How familiar he was with the plea! He knew it word for word: and the incident made a good story for us, receiving such a wide Press distribution, and on so lavish a scale, that, had Mallaig been a burgh, we should have undoubtedly been offered the freedom. Nothing, of course, came of this until the Deluge of War. And then this part of the world developed a sudden strategic importance, and a splendid road is the legacy. This is probably why the Highlander says, with more feeling than any other citizen: 'It takes a war . . .'

One day we repaired the broken cable and floated the canoes in the harbour for any who wanted to sail. At once we had a

20. VIEW FROM ELGOL IN SKYE. *Eigg is on the left, Rhum on the right; Muck is in the distance between them, and far on the left lie the hills of Moidart and Ardnamurchan.*

21. THE *GOLDEN EMBLEM* LEAVES MALLAIG
Sandy Watt, the skipper, is the left-hand figure of the three dark-jerseyed men on the right. In front, hands in pockets, is the fifteen-year-old cook and cabin-boy.

22. THE AUTHOR LEAVING MALLAIG. *The bundle at the stern is the tent, lashed there to break the overtaking waves before they reached the cockpit; even in Mallaig harbour there was plenty of weather, as can be seen here.*

great waiting list, and had to organise the movement. We took a stance at the stone steps under an arch in the pier wall, and standing there all the afternoon, until in the rising tide we were over our knees in water, we launched away citizens and Buchan fishermen, housewives and shopkeepers, and a ration of schoolboys and girls, until at least forty or fifty people had been in each canoe. It was a chilling but pleasant ploy, and we did not stop until everybody who wanted had been out. One or two hardy lads, against orders, went out into the heavy weather beyond the harbour and did quite well. But this was condemned as anti-social by those who still waited.

Among those who sailed were the entire crew of the Gardenstown (Banffshire) drifter *Golden Emblem*. They were over from the east coast for the herring fishing, and were doing no better than any of the others. By mid-morning of the next day we were off with them down towards the Sound of Rhum on the way to the Coll Banks, there to cast our drift nets for the night.

Drift-fishing for herring, a process familiar to us from many trips with Buchan boats, has often been described. The nets are cast late at night until they string out from the bow of the boat a mile in length, floating upright like a net fence just below the surface of the water. In this position the way is taken off the ship, engines stopped, and she drifts for some hours, during which time it is hoped the rising herring are being trapped. They simply have their gills wedged in the inch mesh, and are suffocated. It takes three or four hours to pull the nets in again, whether there is a catch or not. In the normal season this goes on every weekday; out on Monday morning, fish overnight, back and land about dawn, out again, and so on until Saturday.

The *Golden Emblem* was one of the biggest steam-drifters in the fleet; a well-found ship, compared with some of the others. Sandy Watt was her skipper, and he and his younger twin brothers, in the crew, were her chief owners. The ownership was on a share basis by which all profited or lost according to the luck. The ship's company was nine, including the cook, a lad of fifteen who had never been away from home before, and who was sailing—and cooking—without a break during that first four-month season away with the men. Also in the ship, as well as our two selves, was the Watts' father, retired from the sea and harbourmaster of their small native port of Gardenstown.

He was sailing on this trip by way of making a holiday at sea. During the four days Seumas and I were aboard he taught us to mend nets—a graceful art which we were not able to carry beyond the novice stage. First he hung up an old net and slashed his knife downwards through the mesh straight, giving us the task of stringing the sundered parts together by simple stitches with the wooden needle. Then he would slash the net diagonally across, so that our repair had to create stitches running two ways and crossing at right angles. Finally, and hardest, he would cut out a whole section, leaving us to build in a completely new section of net with the needle alone, working inwards from the torn fringes. One needs the fisherman's patience and fortitude for these, and for all the fisherman's tasks.

At this time the herring fishing was a depressed industry. Few boats were making catches; and on those which did there fell the curse reserved in all spheres for the primary producer—poverty prices. The herring, king of fish, has not only ruined crews, and ports, since the start of netting, but, in his aristocratic and capricious wanderings about the seas, has brought down kingdoms. None knows where he comes from, and when he will emerge. It could be that the soundest harvesting and marketing schemes, well financed, adequately safeguarded, with all the equipment and gear necessary to take the prize, and to handle and process and sell and cook it, could tumble—because the herring might simply vanish for an age, as he has done before.

In these years of the middle thirties, successive herring seasons had failed. Most of the share-owning fishermen were in debt—'astern' is their grim description of that condition. Their houses, villas built of granite along the Moray Firth, out of the earnings of forgotten boom years, were mortgaged for bank advances, and fresh debts were being incurred weekly in the Mallaig waters. Crews saved on their own food to buy coal for the drifter engines. Building of boats had stopped; even repairs could not be afforded, and some of the boats, built in the first years of the century, were past repair.

I got an incredible tale of decrepitude when, some months later, I went travelling on behalf of a newspaper round the little herring ports of Buchan. There was no cash about; and although the fee was no more than five pounds for the slipping and dry-docking of a boat to examine her hull, few of the boats had been up on the slip in recent times. In one case, after many trips, a boat was docked, and raised, and the men who examined her stood looking at the sight with the sweat running from them cold. Below the boilers of these small ships a flat bed of cement is spread to protect the hull plates from the heat. In this craft the plates below the boiler had long since rusted away, and, for no one knew how long, she had been sailing on her cement patch!

Other problems of the herring fisher arise from his temperament, the long patient product of his way of life. I have never lived with men more admirable, nor less organised. Like the crofters, they have the perfect neighbourly sense of community, but no instinct whatever for social organisation. They were men, as we have seen them, who after shooting their nets and fighting to draw them again all through a night, getting not a fish; and, heading for home and another trip towards ruination, would stand round on the deck with uplifted caps, upon the belly of the heaving sea, while the skipper offered up a prayer of thanks to God for His goodness and mercy. He must be a jealous God indeed if He does not take pride in the tribute of such splendid sons.

And yet this simplicity made them a prey to the ordinary processes of commerce. In the fish business some of these processes are very ordinary. The fishers had to land their catches, sell quickly, and get away again. They had no bargaining margin, even of time. In glut periods, when there was no sale for the sorely-won catches, they were taken back to sea and thrown away, and the nets put out for more. In a primitive society it is enough to catch fish. The modern fisher had not only to catch but to sell; and if that failed, there was no method by which he could even give them away to the hungry.

During our season there was operating a minimum guaranteed price of ten shillings per cran (of about twelve hundred fish), or ten herrings for a penny. It was an arrangement which appeared to the fishers to realise an impossible dream of security. And it would have been thought that, if such a pitiful price could pay the fishermen, no other dealer could well lose money at the terms. A hitch occurred at once. While there was a guaranteed price, there was no guaranteed sale. And the buyers could readily say 'No!' and condemn more and more of the bounty to be dumped back into the sea.

Other bafflements were also possible. It often happened that a skipper, on coming to port, would be told: 'I can only give you the minimum.' 'I'll take that,' the skipper would say, gladly enough, and put his fish ashore. Then, 'How many crans have you?' would be the question. 'Eighty.' 'Ah, weel, I'm only wanting forty!' It was a dilemma with only one practicable solution. Rather than gather up the unwanted forty crans, and take them back to sea for dumping, the skipper would leave them with the others; and the buyer, paying ten shillings per cran for forty crans, would get the whole catch of eighty for five shillings per cran.

The post-war control schemes and high minimum prices, with graded scales according to the process of food or manufacture intended; the loans for boats and gear; the setting up of more canning and freezing plants; have all brought a high security level to the fisher and his community. But these steps were created by the needs of special times, and the needs will change. In the meantime great markets have been lost, and new ones must be found, not all of them at our own doors. Adjustments must still be made. The present reluctance of some of the fishers to take part in schemes shows the need of an endless good will to mend a long-depressed industry. And behind all these man-made buttresses is the lurking hazard of the herring himself, and the decision he will make, to stay at our shore or to depart.

Whatever commercial or social talents the fishers themselves may lack are more than made up for by their superb seamanlike skill. If there are fish to be caught, they will catch them, and they will sail anywhere to do it. It was in the Kaiser's war that these qualities were brought out into the light. The fishers were an active unit of His Majesty's fleet, and became so because such a high proportion of them had the seaman's instinct for doing the right thing. Between the wars there were drifter skippers and crews sailing our coasts who knew the Adriatic as well as they knew the Moray Firth, having seen Great War service there. Even the Royal Navy had taken them into its service and yet allowed them to do things their own way.

The greatest tribute I ever heard paid to the seamanship of the Navy was spoken by a drifter skipper who did not realise, as he told it, how much his high tribute was, in the by-going, a commendation of himself. He told me: 'They're grand navigators in the Navy', and went on to illustrate this judgment by describing how, in the winter of 1914, he had been told to rendezvous with a destroyer at a certain point in the North Sea. They gave him the bearings, and, in thick fog, he set off from Wick harbour. I can imagine how he would lean out of his wheelhouse, hour after hour, peering into the fog, recognising his road almost by the kent wave-tops. At last, arrived at the spot precisely at the hour and minute arranged, he sounded his siren—and the unseen destroyer sounded alongside him. 'Aye, they're grand navigators in the Navy!' he concluded generously. What he had regarded as normal to himself and his puny craft, he was inclined to think superb professional skill on the part of the destroyer, with her formidable traditions, and braided officers, and their studies and instruments and plottings and well-equipped chart-room.

With men and a ship like these we cast off from Mallaig pier and steamed for the north of Coll. There was the best part of a half south-wester in our teeth, and it was growing. Normally they would not have gone out, but this was already Wednesday; they had been weatherbound since the week-end, and must try for a catch. The Sound of Rhum was a fearsome passage, with Loch Scresort an inviting shelter, and our late Eigg landing-stage at Thuilm now in the lee and showing no breakers.

We brought them no luck. As we cleared the south of Rhum and stood across for the Bank, the sky darkened with the whole savagery of a gale, and we had to turn and run for it, without casting a net. It was a typical courtesy on the part of the skipper (without a thought for the convenience of themselves) that he turned and ran, not for Mallaig, but for Canna, because *we* had never been to Canna.

Another courtesy, on the part of a young crew member at the wheel, while the skipper was below, brought the ship into a moment of danger. The drifter was taking solid water aboard, and I was leaning out of a wheelhouse window, watching for a chance to photograph the decks awash. The helmsman, bent on providing the best available camera material, suddenly, on the approach of an enormous sea, threw her head off. We got the wave below the belt instead of on the shoulder, and rolled on to our beam, until half the deck was under the surface of the water and even the top of the weather rail went out of sight as she staggered back. I lost the deck entirely as it tilted away from me, and got an indifferent picture while hanging in the air by my elbows from the window-ledge. Sandy Watt came splashing up from below and took the wheel in a thunderous silence.

Presently we were skirting into the beautiful bay of Canna harbour. Here we lay at anchor for the characteristic three days of a south-westerly gale, which drove endlessly past the harbour entrance in a black violent curtain, and even in the shelter where we lay stirred us round and round on our cable in a ceaseless fret.

Canna, like Muck, is clean, fertile, smooth, so that one feels a plough could be driven over every inch of the soil. Crofting and lobster-fishing are the mainstays of the few dozen inhabitants. It has no peaks, like Rhum and Eigg, the near neighbours. It is two isles—Sanday, a satellite, and Canna, the mainland. The two enclose the harbour, and approach each other so closely at the inland point that a footbridge connects them—an Atlantic bridge. This little group is the limit of the parish shepherded by the minister and the priest from Eigg. The Roman Catholic chapel is on Sanday; the Church of Scotland on Canna itself. This is a recent building, with a round tower on the ancient pattern serving as a belfry. The door lies constantly unlocked, and the passer-by can drop a coin in the open and teeming collection plate, or even try the harmonium—a harmless musical tribute which I like to permit myself in remote kirks. Sometimes, at Canna, spread out on the green before the church, are to be seen a number of separate jet-black cairns. These are the heaps of coal for the tenants, dumped ashore from the cargo puffer and awaiting carting or ferrying home.

Seumas and I were able to examine the island on this opportune visit. The *Golden Emblem* men launched off their lifeboat for us. We paid visits to a pair of puffers, and to another drifter, storm-bound in the bay like ourselves and glad of a diversion. On a courtesy visit to the laird's house we carried back heavy welcome sacks of potatoes and fresh vegetables, and great broths followed. A launch came alongside one night, with two lobster men, who asked: 'Is it right that you have the Canoe Boys aboard?' We were produced, and to each of us was handed an immense black and agile lobster, with clashing claws, which we received bashfully, and bowed in acknowledgment as the boat backed away from us, leaving us with the armoured bouquets. One of them was the largest lobster any of us had ever seen. They made a superior supper that night, each man with a bolt from the engineer's toolbox set by his plate to crack the shells, and the coal-hammer handy by way of heavy artillery.

By Saturday morning the gale was blowing itself out, and we took up the anchor and ran for Mallaig. In a whole week, not a net had been cast. There was the ship, and her hunger for coal, for nets, for paint, oil, gear. There were ten men, and behind them ten homes. All that the sea had given them in these six fishing days had been the two gift lobsters from the men of Canna.

CHAPTER XV

NORTHWARD

> To magic green shores the horizon is hailing there,
> Luck shall not lack, nor fortune be failing there;
> Give me the sea and soon I'll be sailing there,
>   Swift to the Islands of Glory.
>
> Peace will be sweet when at last I can go to you,
> Then all the seas of the islands I'll show to you;
> There I shall sing all the songs that I know to you—
>   There in the Islands of Glory.

It is probably characteristic of our trip that a chapter bearing the hopeful title 'Northward' should commence with a trip to the southward. Seumas, who made that trip alone, had the best of reasons. For the last two nights aboard the drifter at Canna he had lived in a daze of toothache. When we landed, his jaw was stiff and starting to swell. We got some tea for him and bundled him aboard the midday train for Glasgow, where he might possibly combine some business with relief, if not pleasure. There he sat, in a crowded carriage during the seven-hour journey, and his cheek swelled and puffed into a tight glistening apple whose angry billow sunk his left eye. Passengers sitting opposite stared in a fascination at this display. One of them leaned forward at last and said: 'Excuse me, your face is swelling.' 'I know,' mumbled Seumas sideways.

He tramped the streets of Glasgow that Saturday night, straight from the station, in search of a dentist at home. Late, he stumbled, with his tale of a Highland train journey, into the chair of a man in Partick who tore out the tooth. Recovering in a mist of lifting pain Seumas heard the dentist making small talk with the question: 'You didn't see anything of these canoe chaps when you were up north?' When Seumas had knocked at the surgery door the dentist had been actually reading some newspaper story of ours, and here he was clinking among the very molars of the expedition.

This trip allowed Seumas to pay some Press calls and harry

an editor or two into an even greater awareness of our progress. He also collected overdue payments for stories published, and set off north with some fresh shirts to see us over the last stages.

In the meantime I had been living, quietly and be-kippered, in the now roomier tent, and capturing such photographs as were wanted for publication. The kipper reference is to the main meal of our Mallaig story—warm new kippers, fresh from the ovens and requiring no further cooking. They were made in millions from selected herrings, split and hung from rods, which are latticed in racks up the inside of the kippering sheds: these are merely great hollow funnels of buildings. A loose heap of oak-shavings smoulders on the floor, rising and reeking among the racks of herring and surging in savoury billows from the shuttered roofs. After thirty-six hours of this the kippers are tanned and done—the cheapest and the richest gourmets' food to be had.

'They're bad to beat!' was the tribute of one kipperer, whose palate was in no way dulled by the circumstance that he spent his working life up to the elbows in kippers. The herring, as a food, has this strange regality—that he preserves undiminished the loyalty of those who work for him. No fisher, cooper, gutter, nor kipperer that I ever met had tired of herring. So few herrings were being caught at this season that the normal great contracts were not being filled, and it was easy to glean a few each day for our own kitchen.

With Seumas's return, his face reasonably symmetrical, we were eager to get on. From Mallaig it was to be a pull north up the east coast of Skye in the hope of making the dash over the Minch before the winter hardened. It needed conviction still to believe in this plan, since summer seemed by now to have passed into winter. South-westerly gales ran straight up the Sound of Sleat in their three-day cycle; subsided for a day or two, or only hours; and blasted up again. At night, cold pervaded the tent, and even the inside of the sleeping-bags. We kept sometimes one of the stoves burning low all night, and in the morning would take our first bare footsteps on frosty grass. There was even the conviction of truth in the one or two voices which here, as elsewhere, delivered the warning: 'It's too late in the year!' Even our friends now said something of the sort. 'You've done well enough, boys, and the weather that's been in it this year.

Put these damned canoes on the train and away with them while you're still safe!'

One afternoon we struck camp hurriedly and paddled away from Mallaig. A gale was blowing itself out, but there was still plenty of weather outside, even if it was now more or less with us. There was a very hard press of wind from the west. Once sheltered from the wide open sea by the edge of Skye, we missed the great manageable swell, and got instead smaller fussy breakers.

Nevertheless, Mallaig diminished astern, and we knew that wherever we slept that night, it would not be there. On our right, Loch Nevis ran away in among its growing mountains, and then the shores of Knoydart were pushing at us. To round their westerly boundaries we had to force out into the Sound, until, once past the mainland point opposite Armadale in Skye, we ran free up the coast. The day was already darkening with twilight and rain when, with only a short passage made, we turned in behind the shelter of Airor Island, and landed in a small sea-meadow in the bay beyond.

Here we found a surprising and pleasant little hamlet. There were few houses, and a fine school building, now empty, and needing maintenance to pull it back from the start of decay. When they told us, in the houses, that the school was likely to be closed permanently, we spent the rest of the daylight surveying it, round about the walls and tattered garden, and through the windows. The memory we have of Airor is one of the most compelling of all those we retain. Had it possessed even a serviceable cart-track it would have been still a thriving community; and with a metalled road it would have made a tourist heaven. Lying amongst its green alluvial fields, it looked towards Skye. The view of that rewarding island in the windows of the little school and schoolhouse was as splendid as any we had ever seen from any point of the mainland. Here, if anywhere, one could stay and put to the test those things that otherwise might only be preached of. Here, queerly revealed by a hazard, was the house that one might have vainly sought elsewhere for a year. In these bounds the task of the hands would have dignity and endless self-respect; and, minding the building's first purpose, there might well have been scholarship too. So we proposed and speculated: but we have not yet been back to Airor.

There was a short evening spent in talking to this one and that, and the usual launching and display of the canoes. Rain slanted in heavily with the darkness, and we lay in the tent hoping for an early start with the first light. Later, a swinging lantern came down towards us, and the squelch of boots in the brimming bog at the edge of the meadow. It was a tall young shepherd we had been with earlier, come over to advise the pulling of the canoes in higher above the mark, as the rising wind would pack up the midnight tide and might float them off. He helped us to carry them up, and then was off through the fusillade of rain to his house five miles away at the end of a hill track—a brave figure; a reminder that, whatever switches and fuses and gadgets come to illuminate rural life, much will still depend on the stalwart strong fellow with the swinging lamp.

In the cold of the next morning we paid little attention to the weather, except to note that it was still going roughly in our direction. How roughly, we knew as soon as we forged out from the group of Airor Island and held north-north-east towards the misted distance of Loch Alsh. The Sound of Sleat was white from shore to shore. Skye on our left, and the mainland Glenelg district on our right, formed a narrowing channel up which the weather and the tide gouted, and took us hissing along. The old routine started of the following breakers. We took them with what luck we could, welcoming them under the sterns, riding and fighting them when they burst, and springing for passing new ones, as if they were circus horses, when the previous mount had expired below us. It was brisk work, but it kept us warm and busy, while the familiar hamlets of Skye passed away to port. From that direction also came gusts of wind, diverted by the Skye glens, and hitting us from straight out of the west.

One of these gusts almost ended our journey. We were half a mile south of the Sandaig Islands, heading so that we might slip close round their weather shore and travel on in some shelter under their lee. We were level, fifty yards apart, surfing and bucking, when I heard a shout from Seumas, who was on the mainland side of the channel. All that was to be seen was the bottom of his canoe, turned to me as he skidded on for mad seconds on his right side, and his port blade paddling in the free air above. He had been untwisting himself from the debris of a corkscrewing breaker when a gust, which carried a small extra sea to ram his port side, put him over. With his arm submerged over the shoulder and his face awash he paddled on like a fury with the sunk right blade. He even contrived to feather his blade under water and to keep way on, for a back paddle would have pulled him under. In this way they travelled on their right ear for some unending seconds; then another breaker gathered. The new surge of this one gave Seumas an extra force against which to thrust, and he heaved himself and canoe upright. He came up like a grinning seal, even to the sodden moustache, which had not lately been trimmed. At the sight of me he laughed with great delight. I was gaping in consternation, and shipping water heavily through my open mouth. However, I considered he was entitled to the laugh. The paddle stock had been cracking in his hands as the wood had started to spring with his underwater flailing.

Hereabouts we met other seafarers. A cutter appeared from near Glenelg, and was in sight of us ahead for about half an hour as she made wide and wet tacks southward, pecking across the channel on the wind from shore to shore. She was making very heavy weather of it. Three figures could be seen, and one presently came forward from the cockpit and hung on the weather-shrouds to get a view of us. We could guess her to be a small craft of which we had read, in which some young Danes had undertaken to sail round the world, and which, we learned later that day, had almost been wrecked on the Plock of Kyle, having been towed off its lee shore the previous evening by a Portree fishing skiff. At every plunge of the bow a barrel of sea-water was coming aboard, most of it over the figure at the shrouds. But he stared doggedly until we hailed and waved, when they all waved back. What they saw were two figures waist-high in the sea, wearing red-tooried bonnets and towels for scarves—our winter uniform, as it were. As they passed at twenty yards' distance there was a shouted exchange, and we skipped by them, hearing the drumming of flung water on their close-hauled sails.

Our opposite shore narrowed now to form the channel of Kyle Rhea, while we edged in near the Skye shore to find the smoothest route. Here we expected as much trouble as at the Dorus Mor, and for the same reasons. The tide, as it comes and goes, bores forcibly through this gap, and any small boat in the neighbourhood would rather go with it than try against it. We had, of course, the tide with us, but could recall at least one occasion when that alone was no guarantee of comfort.

The tidal run started opposite Kyle Rhea village, where the facing shores, from being two miles apart, crowd suddenly to a width of a few hundred yards. As if we had slipped over the tilt of a water-shute, we skipped forward, taking the water with us, so that we had to look at the shore to believe we were travelling at all. And to look at the shore, from our level, was to see a revolving blur of rocks and bushes, circling away from us constantly. It was a passage of no terrors; the canoes hardly wagged off their course, and there were whole stretches where paddles could be shipped and the travelling left to the sea, which was so eager itself to quit this squeeze. After three miles the water, grunting with congestion, expanded in a hiss with us into Loch Alsh.

Turning that easterly point of Skye at the perch, we were into water more sheltered from the weather. There was a four-mile plod to Kyle of Lochalsh, and a landing at last below the station pier, on a beach which had positive foothills of sea-wrack. It was here that we met one of our later 'Spanish Armadas', in the shape of an enthusiastic person who came tripping down the jetty to see us, summoning his friends with 'Hurray! Here come the Scandinavians!'

Being in funds to a trifling extent, we installed ourselves for one night in the hotel, where the rain, drumming against our bedroom window, sounded much more threatening than when it smote on our tent. On Skye, now only half a mile across the ferry strait, we had still not landed. But we were this far, and it was easy now. What we should attempt beyond this was something to be decided at once.

Kyle is another Mallaig, in a sense; railway and shipping terminal, ferry point, tourist stage; but with a much smaller stake in the herring industry. Like all the larger Highland communities which are looked at with a close eye, it has its examples of enterprise. The village baker showed us his contribution. The Glasgow bread factories had captured a great Highland trade with wrapped loaves, and this baker had set up a hand-wrapping undertaking of his own. It was a simple device. An iron oven-plate was heating above two paraffin stoves. His loaves, new out of the oven, were wrapped on this slab, the heat being sufficient to seal the ends of the waxed paper. These loaves, infinitely fresher than the Glasgow products, were crossing the ferry by van daily and carrying a local and highly competitive product into the glens of Skye.

The same baker also showed us, perched and clinging securely on a rocky parapet near to his own shop, a strongly fixed fence. It ran round a field of which the fence was a boundary escarpment. The contract of fencing this field had been offered to two separate town contractors, and each, after survey, had turned it down at any price. A local craftsman was persuaded to try it, and he did the job. It is to be remembered that when the Highlander is told to help himself, the task referred to is usually abnormal. He will be criticised for failing to make a road to serve his own village, and one will discover that what is asked for is not a pathway but a mountain goat-track. He will be nagged for not keeping his pier in repair, and will be too polite to request that someone should come and hold back the Atlantic first so that he can get at the job. This is the same citizen who sets casually and eagerly to build a house, plank a boat, or strip an engine—undertakings to baffle even the most intelligent of his town critics. The Highlander has surely got faults enough; but it is time he added to them a sense of impatience with his advisers.

For the sake of being able to write from the actual territory 'we have reached Skye', we paddled over the ferry, landing and drawing up on the stone jetty of Kyleakin. This loveliest village of Skye takes its name from the strait on which it stands, and that kyle of water is called after Haakon, the king of Norway who is also remembered in the name of Kyle Rhea, and whom we met faintly off the island of Kerrera. The Norse left us many names, and little else. One looks for Vikings in vain, although the islesman who most resembled a Viking in my experience was once the ferryman on this very kyle.

Still hopeful of winning at last a break in the weather, and a gentle spell—less than a week would do—to take us up the coast of Skye and place us ready for the Minch crossing, we camped near Mrs. Cameron's tearoom. In that welcoming hostelry we had our meals. In the mornings the daughter of the house would come across the frosty grass and announce: 'Your breakfast's ready!' And, freed for a little time from the oily slavery of the pressure stoves, we would dress and wash, and go in to eat, shivering at first until the first dozen spoonfuls of porridge had gone down. This was pleasant enough, for all our impatience. But the weather did not come. October was waning, and there was never even a tide when we could have gone off hoping to make a useful stage.

Still hopeful of the Minch, we came to a last decision: to travel overland to the north-west corner of Skye, nearest the Outer Hebrides, and to wait there for even one likely day. So for the first time on the trip we dismantled and packed the canoes folded, loading them and ourselves one day on the Dunvegan bus. For five or six hours we swung and jolted, on a road most familiar, across the dear island of Skye—by Broadford, the kyle of Scalpay, Ainort's fiord, round Glamaig to Sligachan, the flight from the Cuillin to Drynoch, the fantastic double loop that takes the road climbing round Braigh Aluinn, the Splendid Hill, with a cheering glimpse to the other shore and the roofs of Talisker Distillery; and so thumping on by Bracadale and Caroy to Dunvegan; where, in the half-dark, we dropped the canoes on ourselves from the bus roof where they had ridden.

That night we slept in the new youth hostel, being the only guests for a week. At our own special request, the neighbouring farmer, who was acting as warden, issued us with six blankets apiece from the store. We needed them, in the great winds and the cold of these days. In the mornings we were no longer baling rain-water from the canoes, but chipping ice out of them. So indoor comforts were necessary, and we had them snugly installed—with the kitchen plenished by our own stoves and pots; the days spent in well-muffled visits here and there; the nights in ceilidhs round our own fire or somebody else's; and a prayer always for the one good day.

But, while awaiting it, the time did not pass without profit. Three letters followed us to Dunvegan, each containing the cheque from one or other of the wholesale newsagent firms which had distributed the *Claymore* for us. These were final payments, but current comforts; and, through the courtesy of the bank manager at Dunvegan, we had soon a sum of about thirty pounds in hand, which was to carry us far.

Apart from the residents of the village, congenial company appeared in the persons of a honeymoon couple. The bridegroom was James Gordon, a Merchant Navy officer whom I had met four years earlier on St. Kilda, a remote part in which to strike up an acquaintance. On that occasion we had sailed with the steamer *Hebrides* to Loch Eport in North Uist, leaving her there to walk across the island together and pick up another steamer at Lochboisdale. In this way we had come to Dunvegan, and he had produced a car from the garage of his summer house there and run me well down the road towards Sligachan, knocking over a cow on the way. He was in the Indian coast service, with home leave only every fourth year. And here we were again, meeting four years later, he with his bride from Cromarty.

One day he drove all four of us to Portree, demonstrating on the way that he had lost none of his steersman's dash. He drove the car like a ship's launch, cornering on the loose stones in a hopping skid, with not the slightest reduction in speed, and hailing: 'Hold tight, passengers! . . . If there's enough water we'll get you off!' Seumas and I, in the rear seat, looked over backwards into valley bottoms which we frequently overhung. But Jim Gordon had sailor's luck, which is the landward equivalent of a soldier's wind. Not only did we get to Portree and safely back, but we visited the famous school there, and had tea in the Carnegie Hostel for the schoolboys. Fifty of them, likely lads gathered from all the Isles, live here as boarders, in the care of a merry band of teachers and a motherly matron. All the boys but four were native Gaelic speakers, and the four, the sons of incoming professional men of various sorts, were learning fast. As the prototype of a residential seminary for young Scots Highlanders, there is certainly a valuable study to be made of this lively place. We learned what we could, so that we were able later to write an article on the Portree School for a weekly paper. It was a production permanently marred by the fact that the paper clapped on to it the unpardonable heading—'The Harrow of the Highlands'.

It was in this hostel that the King and Queen were entertained when they came to Skye on an official visit as Duke and Duchess of York. The luncheon menu, of six or seven courses, was framed on the mantelpiece in the matron's room. It demonstrates a virtue not yet fully realised by the Highland hotelier: every item, except the coffee, had been produced from the soil or the seas of Skye.

At Dunvegan another lesson in self-sufficiency was going

forward, and flourishing before its final collapse. The heiress and chief of all her clan, Mrs. MacLeod of MacLeod, had opened a little egg-testing and grading station, and was making headway with a gallant marketing scheme. It set forth, at that time, with great promise. Eggs stamped 'Dunvegan Tested' were to be seen in Glasgow shops—often the shops of MacLeods (and why shouldn't clan links have a commercial significance!). The crofters of the surrounding countryside sent their eggs; the private bus-owners had agreed, for a good-will send-off to the scheme, to collect and deliver the eggs at half the transport charges. When we visited the egg clearing and packing station Mrs. MacLeod of MacLeod, clan chief of all the MacLeods, had a damp cloth in her hand and was cleaning the crofters' eggs one by one.

The scene was set fair for a practical effort in co-operation. And although the bid failed, probably because the mental climate was not yet favourable, it marked a positive advance towards community enterprise. While it lasted, we made ourselves a non-profit-taking publicity arm, capturing paragraphs here and there for 'Dunvegan Tested'.

Our one good day never came. At night the tin roof of the hostel rattled and lifted in the gale. There was little daylight in the heavy daytime, with the sky, borne down by clouds, the colour of the foaming burns. A decision came in the last week of October. It was time to make another forward move, as clearly as we could see. One day we simply packed up our log and charts, and the trip was over.

Towards that evening the steamer *Loch Broom* came into Dunvegan pier, southward-bound from Ullapool to the Clyde by way of Tobermory. We carried the canoes aboard her, hoping to be at Calve in the morning. Dunvegan Head was hardly cleared before the weather hit us as if the previous three months had been merely practice. And, big ship as she was, she ran staggering into Loch Pooltiel, to huddle at anchor for two days. In spite of the steerage tickets we had bought, and the fact that we assembled our stoves in sheltered corners of the alley-ways and made tea and brose at intervals, the steward permitted us to sleep on the cushions of the smoking-room after the other passengers had gone to their cabins.

There were, however, few passengers. Apart from ourselves,

there were only four, all of them men. Three of them were obvious tourists, making a last end-of-season adventurous trip into the wilds. Their garb was aggressively nautical, with peaked caps or berets, reefers, and mighty cable-stitched sweaters. The other was a tall *soigné* figure, incongruously outfitted in stylish dark tweed overcoat, bowler hat, pointed shoes, and carrying kid gloves and a rolled umbrella. Thus he strolled the deck firmly, with a brisk word here and there and a knowing eye up into the weather. It was a sight rarely to be seen on a cruising and cargo steamer, and his fellow-passengers of the saloon, among themselves, found in him a subject for some hearty seafaring drolleries.

We discovered that the man in the bowler was less of a misfit than he appeared. It was the steward who told us that he was one of the senior Clyde pilots, taking a late fortnight of leave, in the outfit which he undoubtedly considered gave him the most contrasting holiday feeling. On one occasion he took off his gloves to play a dapper practical joke upon a passenger who had a fishing line over the stern as we lay at anchor. While the fisher was below, discussing a glass of whisky, the pilot pulled in the line and fixed to the hook the form of a fish which he had cut out in tin, with shears borrowed from the bo'sun. The hauling in of this catch was an enjoyable diversion.

Another of the passengers was a Ministry of Labour official, seeking respite from the sorrows of attempting to settle unemployed city lads on the land, and to persuade them of the difference in working conditions between farms and factories. He told a story, heavy with frustration, of one reluctant recruit, listening to a plea that Saturday and Sunday also brought their farm tasks, who interrupted with: 'Listen, mister—I wouldnae work on Setturday afternoon for Jesus Christ!'

In two days the weather abated to a normal south-wester, and we heaved down the coast of Skye, and southwards towards Ardnamurchan, which the canoes seemed to have passed so long since. Neither of us was to see these parts again until the following year, when Seumas would complete the first intention of the trip and cross a stormy Minch alone, a tiny and solitary figure. It was to be an effort which seems to me to remain the best single feat of canoeing in British waters.

But now, steamer-borne, we made such a slow wallow round Ardnamurchan Point that the ship felt sick, as if she would be glad to founder and have done with it. In a long time, with Ardmore abeam, we had a little shelter, and at last, there was the end of Calve!—and the bump when we embraced Tobermory pier.

As we paddled over the bay towards the island we came under the familiar stern of the *Hebrides*, lying at her anchor for a night of shelter. Alastair MacRae, her radio operator, who now radio-operates aircraft round the world, came to the stern and spoke to us in wisdom and relief: 'God, are you still alive? Go home now and burn these dam' canoes.'

CHAPTER XVI

THE HIGHLAND PROBLEM RESOLVED

> Fate to a task has willed us,
>   (Weaker is Fate than men!)
> To-morrow the fear that chilled us
> Burns in the fire that filled us—
>   Careless of where and when
> To-morrow our hands shall build us
>   Power and pride again.

ANYONE who is prepared to set down a plan for the solution of the Highland problem must be aware of plenty of past and present competition. There are not enough pigeon-holes in Whitehall to accommodate the plans which have been made for the Highlands. It is an old story. Sincere men and committees have been publishing reports and recommendations for two hundred years. There was one common flaw in these plans. None of them conceded that Scotland, as a nation and an economic unit, must be the whole basis of the solution.

Our solutions are of a simple if whole-hearted character. First, the planning must be conceived and done from Scotland, although the lack of such an authority should not delay their starting. If Holland had remained a Spanish colony, who in Madrid would have cared much about the need for a fight to win back Walcheren from the sea in 1946?

It was a point which we were able to see clearly when we made a tour among the industries of rural Ireland a summer or two later. The urgent need in Ireland had been to create employment outlets for the youth of the large country families who could not all gain a living from the family holding. To achieve this quickly, direction of industry had been put into force on an almost fey scale. Factory enterprises and light industries, many of them inspired from abroad with refugee capital, were ushered into remote corners of the country, often with odd results; like the factory for women's hats in Galway, claimed to be the most up to date in Britain, which overnight launched the daughters of the Claddagh fishermen into the making of Parisian creations under the direction of a Viennese milliner of European reputation. What impressed us about the young men who were administering these schemes was that they were not working in a cemetery of dead Reports. They were too busy to find out that the job could not be done.

The key solution to the Highland problem is transport and communications. After that comes the use of the land and its assets, for the first time in a modern and efficient setting. That is the whole story.

Transport and communications throughout the Highlands and the Isles must be geared to the needs of these communities. If one could travel, or transmit goods and information at will, between one West Highland point and another, almost everything that could be desired in development would follow surely after. A system of transport is useless that is conceived as the hinder end of a pattern radiating outwards from the 'Home Counties', and designed in the first place to speed north the escaping man of wealth and his gun-dogs. The whole transport plan must be modelled anew to serve the people of the place, and those others who will come, or come back. They must be enabled—especially those on the western seaboard—to move readily among the neighbouring townships, and to shift their goods out and in at a commercial pace. If this is not their right as British citizens—and it has certainly not been so up to now—then it will be their amenity as natives of an area which must be the object of a national investment for the national profit and well-being. Coastal linking by sea, now neglected except for steamers making calls at widely scattered points, must play a large part in this. The coastal activity of Norway, with hundreds of small vessels always on the move, shows something of what can be accomplished when transport is treated as a people's service and not as an outpost incidental.

The developing of a smooth transport system would at once increase the industry of tourism, to which the Highlands can rightly look as one of its great by-products. It was a mordant joke with Seumas and me, as we worked our strenuous way north, that we had always been conscientious proselytes for a long

Highland tourist season; and we so remained throughout our trip, mentioning in our weather-beaten journalism that the area was ideally designed for late and early season holidays. We stuck to the point until the end. Our year was not typical, and there are ample temperature and sunshine records to make the case. July and August tend to be the wet months. May and early June are lovely, and in the back end of the year the mild days run on, forgetful of winter, often until after Christmas.

We shall be looking later at the means by which the Highlander's temperament might be adjusted to his future. He has a shyness, about what he imagines to be his amenity shortcomings, which has stultified the growth of a holiday-making industry, and has disappointed many would-be tourists and friends. He has persuaded himself that no visitor will stay under a roof which does not shelter a bath with hot and cold running water, or other lavish plumbing for which adequate substitutes are available. It is a grievous error, and in the past it has prevented many young persons from the joy of living in a Highland home. There is some gentle corrective work to be done here. The wayside cottages along the English main roads have done better, with their little cards saying 'Teas' or 'Bed and Breakfast —5/6'. The Highlander has been diverted from the great rewards of a popular holiday industry by the thought of the well-to-do sportsman in the big hotel, hiring his gillies and dressing for dinner.

There are some who see in a tourist industry a danger of a national devotion to flunkeyism. Switzerland is readily quoted as a country largely committed to tourism. It is wholly wrong, however, to imagine that the Swiss have required to become a nation of hotel boots and valets. They have taken, almost as a personal and national challenge, the need to turn their hands, perhaps by way of contrast, to some high craftsmanship. In witness of which they have their superb watch industry, setting itself probably the highest standard of precision tool-work in the world. But in addition, their tourist industry seems to have been so devised as to admit to full opportunity their splendid engineers, with their hydro-electric power, and the endless installations of mountain railways, lifts, lake steamers, for which tourists willingly pay extremely heavy charges.

These Swiss undertakings are the result of a community

impulse—a virtue which has not yet inspired many of the Highland tourist efforts. The inward tendency to security still stands in the way of even small efforts to beautify the community. While houses are spotless inside, gardens are rare—although becoming less so. Village efforts towards the creation of some such communal asset as a sports field or a hall have failed more often than they have succeeded. There are signs of a leadership which might well provide the trifling impetus required to break this social diffidence. One minor but essential tidying-up which could touch-off the springs of action in any village I can think of would be a bid to tidy up the place, and stop, for example, using the harbour as a rubbish dump.

The design of a tourist industry must also have a Scottish context. One piece of post-war planning has already been a monstrous witness to the errors of centralisation. The Catering Wages Acts, designed perhaps to protect the staffs of hotels in the West End of London, became a strangling menace when applied to the small family hotels of the Highlands, and presumably of similar districts. Not for the first time, rural Britain carried Mayfair on its back.

But it is to the land that the Highlands must look—this time with promise—for their salvation. In the course of its long evolution the West of Scotland produced for its own needs the system of crofting, based on the most perfect utilisation of the land and sea assets of the district, without modern techniques, which had yet been devised. The basis of crofting is the small family land-holding, providing a food and clothing subsistence, with the head of the family employed seasonally or part time in a cash-earning employment. Any scheme to 'better' the present-day Highlander must follow this model, which is founded on the individual, and on control from within the community. Whatever immense changes may come, either to the Highlands or to the cities, it is likely that for a great period forward into our history there will be fringes of community life, around the west, still holding to this ancient way of life.

It will be one of the most exciting social experiments of our times to apply to this pattern and technique of living, the scientific training of our recent years. There is already a considerable outward pressure from the cities, to carry back into the country the technical skills which have been building up in urban industry. Country revolutions, even social ones, have always derived their leadership from the towns: even from their own kin in the towns, who have shared origins but have shed inhibitions.

This first battalion of town recruits, refreshed by new skills and associations, is ready. Their names are listed in the cardindexes of applications for crofts and small holdings filed in the Department of Agriculture offices in Edinburgh. And familiar names they are—hardly a foreign or even a Lowland name among them. It runs to many thousands of able applicants, and it reads like a clan muster-roll for Prestonpans. All of them are seeking back, with a true instinct, to the heartening sources and resources of their own places. It will not, of course, be necessary to have these returning townsmen become crofters on the old pattern. The time has come to allow subsistence crofting to develop into a more efficient and specialist farming, in large or small cultivation units according to the ability of the man and the ground.

It is part of the dramatic expectation of all Highland concerns that this leadership, and this specialism, are already in view. Here and there about the territory already one sees emerging the landowner himself, in the rôle—not common in recent Scotland—of the laird who is determined to make the land abound. These are young men. Some of them have ancient clan associations with their land. Others are more recently in possession. It is to be remembered that in the whole of broad Scotland one would have difficulty in finding a laird who speaks like a Scotsman. It requires a belief in historic justice to understand the strange divagations which bring them to their present tasks by way of Eton, Oxford, the Guards, and all the rest. It may be that some are attracted to nurture their own lands by heavy post-war taxation and the belief that the firm outlook for British agriculture offers the best commercial proposition of the generation; it may be that some of them feel moved by the stirring which Scotland has been experiencing. But, whatever the motives, here they are, emerging suddenly, with the promise of leadership in the form most fitting to the hour. Under their hands, new soil and crop and cattle-rearing theories are in for a brisk time, and are already showing profit.

It is in the scale of this movement that the most confidence is wanted. The petty patching and scraping, which has been all we have to show for Highland planning, must be altogether laid aside. The scene is set for a great, costly, and early-profitable investment. Camping in lost and lovely sea-valleys, Seumas and I used to envisage (in those days of great unemployment) an army of men moving over the land; fitted with mechanical weapons of reclamation, and all the other needed tools; clearing the jungled ground, road-making, draining, ditching, fertilising, fencing, improving, setting the soil in order; building the houses and the byres; moving on, and dropping behind them, into restored and present-day communities, men from this rescuing army. It seemed reasonable to imagine that thus could have been created probably the most efficient and profitable food-production countryside in the world. It was then, to many, a wild and romantic dream. Since then, proofs are ample that there is no practical impossibility in all this; and if it be still a dream, whoever says so must be prepared to explain away a plan of neglect to a defrauded people. Too many have witnessed immense dubious schemes, sponsored by Government for food development abroad, to believe that there are no resources to invest in food production on a big scale at the back door.

So far as the Highlander is concerned, there will be a need to move him towards the state of mind where he can readily take part in co-operative enterprise for the district and the national weal. He is not yet ready for the setting of a modern community. One finds oneself using the word 'modern' with insistence. It is not a modern world in which the Highlander lives. I have explained most of the reasons for this. Very little of the fault is his. But he will quickly and willingly learn, given the right start. The right start will be a double process of education.

In the first place, he requires to see demonstrated under his eyes the practicability of the new methods by which all his standards can be raised. Demonstration farms and crofts, electrical gadgets worked with power from the new hydro-electric schemes, trial forestry plantings—all on his own soil and not in some distant agricultural laboratory—these are the constant need.

There is also the difficult process of putting the Highlander's inward temperament in tune with the march of events. We have here something to learn from the field work of the St. Francis

Xavier University at Antigonish, which, aided by the Canadian government departments, has carried out some valuable experiments in adult education among the crofting-fishing communities of Nova Scotia. This province has had much in common with the recent history of the Highlands. Its small villages and hamlets have been subject to constant economic pressure from the more populous areas, and for the past several generations, active young people have been creamed off by the attractions of employment in distant industry, leaving an ageing and not over-enterprising population. The self-help schemes initiated by the St. Francis Xavier instructors took the form of preparatory village discussion groups, from which rose a recognition of the need for faith and investment in the local resources. Communal savings schemes led to the founding of such schemes as co-operative buying agencies, or canning factories, where surplus fish or fruit—previously waste—could be prepared for a non-perishable market. It is claimed that not only have the resulting schemes prospered and flourished, bringing morale as well as profit, but that local leaders have emerged in all communities, among young people who could not make themselves felt in the old state of society. There is enough evidence to warrant a study of this work with an eye on Scottish application.

A constant need is to keep up the standards at which the Highlands should aim in selling what they have to offer. The large tweed industry was forced to high standards through competition in world markets. In other directions there has been no improvement over the years. Those who deplore the loss of the former enormous overseas markets for barrels of cured salt herring never mention what seems to me the most prominent feature of this product—that an open barrel of salt herring is one of the most repellent spectacles in the whole range of human food. The herring industry is only now painfully catching up with modern canning and processing methods without which it will simply not live.

This is a factor to be borne in mind by the well-meaning organisations which are doing good enough work in finding market outlets for the spare-time work of crofters—knitted goods and the like. The tendency has been in the past to organise these on a charity basis, so that the public might respond to appeals to buy the output of the struggling crofters. Under such a system, standards are no higher than might be expected. Hand-knitted socks and hose, for example, will be ill-matched in size; made from coarse yarns, and drab in colouring.

We believed that this was the wrong approach, to this as to most other Highland problems, and we set out to prove it. We were sure that Highland women could knit more attractively than they were asked to do under the system, and that their dyes could also be made in gay colours which would not require a charity incentive in the public which might buy them. If the standard could be pushed up, there would be no need to sell the articles on a charity basis. Among the five of us who formed the original *Claymore* band we scraped together a tiny capital which enabled us to set up a non-profit-taking marketing organisation with an attic office in Glasgow. We offered to the crofter women prices which were at least double those which were offered elsewhere. More than half of the first lots had to be rejected out of hand. They had all the faults which went uncorrected by the patrons of the other system. The initial cost of return postage on parcels almost ruined us. But slowly, by degrees, standards went up. Socks grew to the same size of foot and leg—a novelty hitherto. We designed mountaineering, ski and walking and fishing socks and mitts, with what bachelor struggles may be imagined. Bright reds, greens, blues, they came at last—softly and expertly finished, with forgotten and complex decorations knitted into the tops. Modern sports stores were eager to have these. We sold as many as we could commission, and at prices more than double those which our competitors asked retail for their distressing products. All the profits went back into increased payments to the knitters. Into one tiny island of the Outer Hebrides went a steady flow of money during the last winter before the war. By the summer of 1939 our goods were selling in the leading sports shops of the West End of London, in direct competition against similar Swiss and Norwegian products, the expert output of the people who had invented this specialised market.

On the outbreak of war we had to wind up the business, as we were all to be far sundered. It has not, of course, been possible to have a hand in any such undertaking since; and from what one can see the standards have lapsed to what they were at our beginning. To some, it will seem fantastic that the setting on foot of a brief practical experiment like this should be solely the spare-time task of a few young men without backing or authority. If that is the impression, those who have it know little of the major fantasies of the Highland problem; and of the studied neglect and betrayals which have gone to make it. For us the venture was valuable in that it showed the job could be done: and that the Highlander, given the goal and the impetus, could do it.

All the proofs are there; the experiments are all done; there is a successful technicological answer to all the claims that 'it can't be done': 'the land is useless': 'the people won't work': 'it's too late in the year'. If the British people and their nourishment is a present concern, the proofs are overwhelming for a confident investment of faith and works. Not a tenth part will be necessary of the faith which inspired any one phase of the development of the Empire, of which the Scotland of the Highlander is a mother-country. There is not a part of this Empire but would rejoice in its blood stream to see the Highlander, armed with the resource which he has displayed in every spot but where his heart lies, enter upon a new and splendid season of fruitfulness.

CHAPTER XVII

'IT'S TOO LATE IN THE YEAR'

> No rest from restless will
> And hot desire,
> We take the tide at the fill
> Tho' the gale's higher,
> Knowing, when winds grow still,
> So does the fire.

THE ropes were stiff with ice as we coiled them aboard the Calve rowing-boat and pushed off into the Sound. I sat in the bow, holding fast the packed canoes, and Seumas and Calum had an oar apiece. It was black dark, with dawn more than an hour away. A mile over at the pier of Tobermory, with all her ports and decks lit, was the Oban steamer, the *Lochinvar*. We could hear clearly her engine-room telegraph as the bridge spoke to those below. She would sail in fifteen minutes, taking us south.

Calve dwindled astern, the kitchen light pouring on to the front grass, and the girls at the end of the jetty with the lantern waving. As we came alongside the *Lochinvar*, she swung open her side doors and hauled in Seumas and me, and then the canoes, with Calum boosting them up from the boat. The steamer was moving almost at once, so that we had time only to run to the top deck and hail Calum finally as the darkness took him. Once out in the Sound of Mull, the *Lochinvar* hammered down the strait to Oban, and the sky brightened towards the day.

Waiting for the dawn, we found it took an effort to look ahead and speculate on what was next for ourselves. For months now, we had hardly looked farther into the future than the next day. We did not know that our immediate future was to be a hungry winter in London; but it was a prospect which would not have greatly troubled us.

What we did know, beyond all uncertainty, was that not this

nor any other dawn would ever show us here a profitless land—a permanently beautiful but barren waste. It was, on the contrary, a rich land, if neglected; fertile in all but faith. This was what we had set out, hopefully, to see. And the discovering of it, and the proving of it, at least to ourselves, and the telling of the story as we went, was gain enough. Even if there were never to come our way again a chance to carry the conviction a point onward, we should have something in our recalling of these days to answer any who might ask: 'But what came of it?'

It would be too extravagant, doubtless, to claim a large influence in the new mood which informs the whole question of rural, especially Highland, development. For all the neglect it has endured, there is almost enough strength rooted in our countryside itself to produce the seeds of its own salvation. But it is not ungrateful to think that, in those bankrupt times, we were at least in the right place.

In a narrower field, there was clearly an achievement to be claimed—whether we were the whole cause or not. From the time of our endeavours, the fairy tale and clan gossip-monger as such has been discredited—or, at least, dismissed to his proper paltry position among the social literature of the times. It has become necessary to discuss the present-day country in terms of the modern citizens. It is a slow process; but the recording of the Highlanders and their activities as members of adult communities, and not as mere remnants and salvage of a past, is the first real step forward out of the fey background to which the guide-book romanticist damned them. This one step is more important than any other.

Lest such thinking should make us preen, that morning on the way down the Sound of Mull, the sun spilled up into daylight, throwing gold ablaze on the sea and all the bracken hills. The steamer cracked the water, splintering it like a mirror, as it lay smooth and unmoved before our bows, and all round from shore to shore.

It was the first windless day since we had started out from Bowling on the Clyde almost three months before. It was a day when a canoe could have gone anywhere. The middle of the Minch would be glassy, where we could have bathed and swum, and crossed at our leisure from side to side and back again in one sunlight.

Such days come to the West late in the year, like opportunities; and when they come, he who has had patience will do everything. In these places, it is never too late in the year. Opportunities abound, and all things are possible, even to those who may not wait for calm weather.

Ingram Content Group UK Ltd.
Milton Keynes UK
UKHW011412170723
425287UK00001B/73